1981

WALTER PATER'S ART OF AUTOBIOGRAPHY

# *Walter Pater's Art of Autobiography*

GERALD MONSMAN

Yale University Press New Haven and London

Designed by James J. Johnson
and set in VIP Palatino type.
Printed in the United States of America by
Vail-Ballou Press, Binghamton, N.Y.

*Library of Congress Cataloging in Publication Data*
Monsman, Gerald Cornelius.
    Walter Pater's art of autobiography.
    Includes index.
    1. Pater, Walter Horatio, 1839–1894.  2. Auto-
biography.  3. Fiction, Autobiographic.  4. Authors,
English—19th century—Biography.  I. Title.
PR5136.M64    824'.8  [B]  80–11941
ISBN 0–300–02533–5

1 2 3 4 5 6 7 8 9 10

*To My Children*

# Contents

# Acknowledgments

I am indebted for much of the intellectual inspiration for this study to the fiction and criticism of J. L. Borges and John Barth and, in particular, to the critical theory and practice of J. Hillis Miller and Harold Bloom. Grateful acknowledgment is also made to those who read and helpfully commented upon this study in manuscript, both for the Yale Press and for the Duke University Research Council. Acknowledgment is also made to *Nineteenth-Century Fiction* for permission to use portions of "*Gaston de Latour* and Pater's Art of Autobiography," 33 (1979): 411–33, and to *Victorian Studies* for permission to use "Narrative Design in Pater's *Gaston de Latour*" (forthcoming, Spring 1980), as well as to Sharon Bassett for allowing me to quote from several unpublished manuscripts of Pater at Harvard's Houghton Library. Finally, the Duke Research Council is thanked for kindly making available for this study a publication subvention.

# Introduction

"Where are the dead? Nowhere!" Sometimes I try to imagine these startling words as having been spoken by one or another of Walter Pater's doomed heroes. But I cannot— almost, perhaps, but never quite. These uncharacteristically self-revelatory lines (written by Pater in the summer of his nineteenth birthday just as his family was dispersing and he was about to leave King's School for Oxford) belong to no figure in any of the portraits save the author himself—in the midst of a crisis of faith, deeply disturbed at having lost the assurances of conventional belief, and longing for an abso- lute Truth and some transcendent refuge:

> Now life is all in all, yet come it will
> That tragedy of death in sternness dread,
> To check long-cherished hopes, old passions still,
> A dark and silent void. Where are the dead?
> Nowhere!—a voice replies. Yet Thou hast died,
> Oh Christ Redeemer! Let me cling to Thee,
> Hold me from yon abyss; with frenzied glide
> Down, down I sink. Oh! let me live in Thee,
> Or deep in hell,—it seems so awful not to be.
>
> And yet in dreams at night, in wakeful dreams
> When thought is free and flings her bonds away,
> The soul untrammeled like a prophet seems
> To tell how all things verge to their decay;
> Herself, that seems immortal, in the round
> Of nature—mistress stern—shall one day fall

Back whence she came, nor hear the trumpet sound
Awakening, nor the high Archangel's call
And chaos grim once more supremely rule o'er all.[1]

"Watchman, what of the night?" had begun with a four-stanza description of a stormy night and the coming of dawn, but here in the stanzas quoted it turns inward and all but denies to the soul its corresponding dawn. Although "Watchman" concludes with two strongly orthodox stanzas affirming the writer's hope of resurrection, the conventional imagery and sentiment ring hollow. Pater's early biographer, Thomas Wright, described it as a religious poem. But one may say of this juvenile piece precisely what T. S. Eliot had remarked of Tennyson's *In Memoriam*: it is religious not "because of the quality of its faith, but because of the quality of its doubt. Its faith is a poor thing, but its doubt is a very intense experience."[2]

Proposing to his publisher an early series of autobiographical portraits, Pater had remarked of the first installment: "I call the M.S. a portrait, and mean readers, as they might do on seeing a portrait, to begin speculating—what came of him?"[3] After his teens, what became of this doubting lad of "Watchman" is a story that merits retelling—how (to quote Philip Toynbee's pithy sketch) at the high tide of Victorian moral earnestness Pater, now a young fellow of Brasenose,

hurled down an almost contemptuous challenge to the whole of educated English society. He had announced

1. Pater, "Watchman, what of the night?" stanzas 7, 8 (1858), quoted in Germain d'Hangest, *Walter Pater: L'homme et l'oeuvre* (Paris: Didier, 1961), 1: 343 n. 25.
2. Eliot, "In Memoriam," *Selected Essays: New Edition* (New York: Harcourt, Brace, 1950), p. 294.
3. *Letters of Walter Pater*, ed. Lawrence Evans (Oxford: Clarendon, 1970), p. 30.

that aesthetic passion ought to be given priority over ethical values, social conventions and religious faith; a claim which must have been as astonishing as it must have seemed bold and original. . . . But during the later seventies the rebel began to suffer the inevitable consequences of his audacity: he was passed over for academic advancement; he was made to feel the hostility of the university establishment in many other ways; he began to be thundered against in the intellectual reviews. By 1882 we find that the "W. H. Pater" who had scandalised his seniors and delighted so many of his contemporaries and juniors, has suddenly evaporated, to be replaced by that old pussy-cat "Walter Pater" with whom posterity has been so much more familiar. Living in North Oxford with his two maiden sisters, taking tea, making cautious expeditions to Italy, corresponding courteously but anaemically with minor literary acquaintances, the new Pater became almost a joke for his old-maidishness and severe propriety.[4]

Such a portrait vividly captures the droll superficies of Pater's life—that metamorphosis of doubt into a creed which others, more willing than Pater to play the decadent, celebrated long after he had opted for respectability by a kind of self-cancelation.

One might, however, better answer the question "What came of him?" by analyzing those fictional forms in which Pater characteristically expressed his yearning for a refuge from the threatening "abyss." About 1887–88 he seems to have faced a creative crisis that caused him to abandon at midpoint the autobiographical "trilogy" he had begun with

4. Toynbee, "Rebel into Pussycat," review of *Letters*, ed. Evans, *Observer* (London), 16 August 1970, p. 21.

4 INTRODUCTION

*Marius the Epicurean* (1885) and was continuing in *Gaston de Latour* (1888–). The origin of this crisis lay in the childhood loss of both Pater's father and mother, a dreaded yet desired separation from parental dominance that left an indelible sense of guilt and remorse for having somehow caused or willed their deaths. Pater dealt with this guilt by a textual sublimation or displacement, exorcising his conflicting emotions through the act of autobiography. There, in the text, the paternal figure, reembodied as any preexisting work or critically conservative dogma, is slain so that the younger, as the autobiographical author of his life, might endow himself with that paternity for which as a child he had insatiably yearned. But when in 1887 the death of his elder brother William had summoned that old sense of triumph and remorse for the third time in Pater's life, the public autobiographical assumption of paternity could no longer appease the private guilt. Owing to the hostility of critics who irrevocably linked him with those errant sons, his decadent disciples, Pater balked at taking upon himself the role of father. Because there could be no satisfactory public exchange of roles, there could be no private discharge of the burden of blood-guilt, and "the hand collapses."

The relation between Pater's private psychological drama and the form or structure of his fiction is a shared reflexiveness: the turning of the child back upon the parent is echoed in the multiple levels of the reflexive text turning back perpetually upon each other. Although Pater's persistent interest in such figures as Thackeray, George Eliot, and Browning suggest that he found in their work tendencies quite similar to his own—the "reflexive" indirections of Thackeray in *Henry Esmond*, the mythic deconstruction of linear history in Eliot's *Middlemarch* and *Daniel Deronda*, the search for multiple selves through Renaissance masks conducted by Browning—yet more than any other Victorian Pater succeeded, by heroic force of intellect spurred on by the most painful of psychological urgencies, in giving a new emphasis to the point of view involved in the act of artistic creation; that is, to the processes and problems of consciousness and to the activities of reading and composition as themselves the subjects of fiction. In this, Pater inevitably seems something of an anomaly as a Victorian, a transitional figure who was in, but no longer of, the nineteenth century. But against whom, then, should he be scaled if not his contemporaries? The immediate answer—the "old masters" of twentieth-century fiction, Conrad, Joyce, Woolf—is certainly not wrong; but it would be more exciting to see Pater as a figure impressively bridging the gap between romanticism and postmodernism, between nineteenth-century fictional models and those ultrareflexive writers whose fictional worlds invariably lead back to the generative activity of art itself: Borges, Beckett, Robbe-Grillet, Leiris, Nabokov, Fowles, Barth, Barthelme, to name several. What these writers openly proclaim (a bit shrilly at times) Pater had whispered elegantly but urgently: language does not merely imitate reality but creates it.

My intention here is not to demonstrate Pater's specific influence on any later writer or writers but in a broad way simply to isolate within his work the same themes of artistic self-consciousness as are present in contemporary literature. Pater's recognition that the categories of space, time, matter, identity, causation, and memory are tentative, incomplete, arbitrary, and relative dictates a unique kind of fiction that swallows up veridical reality. Thus, rather than attempting a veridical illusion of life, Pater's writings, like those of contemporary writers, affirm the autonomy of their artifice—artifice being, indeed, their meaning—and the various narrative devices that call attention to the work's fictiveness are strategies for replacing an elusive outer reality with a self-

sustaining imaginative reality. Nowhere in his fiction did
Pater attempt to conjure up the plot excitement of battles,
passions, and escapes by sharply visualized action (*vide*
Charles Kingsley, Edward Bulwer-Lytton, or Lew Wallace),
for that sort of popular historical romance was in his estima-
tion mere antiquarianism.[5] It was not Pater's regnant intention merely to describe actions directly (he contemptuously
refers in *Marius* to "the long shows of the amphitheatre"
which were, "so to speak, the novel-reading of that age—a
current help provided for sluggish imaginations" [*Marius*, 1:
239];[6] nor did he propose to be openly autobiographical, to
allow himself what would be, even were it justified, a very
painful form of direct self-revelation. Instead, he discarded
conventional mimetic assumptions in favor of a reflexive
textual model. The Paterian text is a ceaseless shuttling back
and forth between all possible levels: historical fact and literary myth, preexisting texts, its own plot and sense of composition, the author's autobiographical stance, the reader's experience in the 1870s or 1880s, the critic's writings in the
present. As beauty and horror, life and death, ceaselessly
pass into each other across the "abyss" of a mutually sustaining, ordering, and enhancing dialectic, Pater approaches
asymptotically that decentered reality reflected within the
text's play of differences.

   In recent years much attention has been given to Victorian autobiography, centering primarily, so far, on the more

   5. "In handling a subject . . . anything in the way of an actual revival
must always be impossible. Such vain antiquarianism is a waste of the
poet's power." Instead, the artist "vitalizes his subject by keeping it always
close to himself." Pater, "Poems by William Morris," *Westminster Review*,
NS 34 (1868): 307, 306.
   6. Parenthetical citations made within the text are to the Library Edition
of *The Works of Walter Pater*, 10 vols. (London: Macmillan, 1910); these citations are shortened to only the page number if they follow a previous reference to the identical work.

overt autobiographical acts of a Newman or a Ruskin or a Mill. But Pater's overriding strategy is to reveal himself covertly by deploying through critical or fictionalized critical utterances "a self not himself" (2: 67). The reflexive text is thus a mirror in which Pater causes his own image, inscribed within the textual apparatus, to turn back upon the image of his hero and his hero's age—which then, once again, turns back upon the author's life.[7] To illuminate this elusive relationship between the author and his text, I have deemed it necessary to alternate the discussion of psychological themes with textual ones. To that end, the first chapter, "Criticism as Creation," considers how Pater's role as critic extends to the inscription of himself within the works of other writers, those writers being Pater's own dialectical double. The second chapter, "Visionary Texts," specifically analyzes how Pater's first three works—*Studies in the History of the Renaissance* (1873), *Marius the Epicurean* (1885), and *Imaginary Portraits* (1887)—are able to locate a visionary wholeness in place of that "abyss" of the disintegrating flux. The third chapter, "Parent and Child," examines the biographical un-

7. "Academic criticism works very hard to depersonalize its insights, to mask its fears and wishes in a language of secure authority. As readers, we must come face to face with the conflict behind that mask. . . . Part of the pleasure of reading criticism is experiencing the subtle ways in which the biases, hopes, and frustrations of the critic are woven into the texture of his language and even into the language of the texts he examines. This dialectic between self and other, embedded in the critic's language and method, is really what criticism is 'about.' There is no way a critic can simply talk about history without trying to engage and co-opt it. . . . As Northrop Frye has written, 'there is always a sense in which criticism is a form of autobiography. . . .' But autobiography, especially if we conceive it as unconscious motivation, will not be sufficient to account for the act of writing criticism. . . . No critic's personality will be merely reproduced in his criticism; instead, it will undergo a compromised, purgative fulfillment in the interaction between the texts he has read and the text he is writing." Cary Nelson, "Reading Criticism," *Publications of the Modern Language Association* 91 (1976): 803, 804, 815, 809.

derpinnings of Pater's search both to find his selfhood in
other figures and to inscribe this doubling within self-sustaining structures in which the simulacra of past and present experience are reified. The fourth chapter, "The Abandoned Text," then considers the unfinished *Gaston de Latour*
(1888–) in which all the psychological urgencies that have
built up over a lifetime finally overwhelm and paralyze Pater.
Finally, the fifth chapter, "Beauty and Evil," finds in Pater's
last fictional works, "Emerald Uthwart" and "Apollo in
Picardy," covert commentaries on just why in *Gaston* the
autobiographical trilogy could go no further.

# CHAPTER ONE

# Criticism as Creation

Thanking William Sharp for an early and enthusiastic review of *Marius the Epicurean*, Pater confessed: "Such recognition is especially a help to one whose work is so exclusively personal and solitary as the kind of literary work, which I feel I can do best, must be."[1] In his posthumous tribute to Pater in 1894, Sharp elaborated on this "personal" quality in Pater's work:

> There are few more autobiographical writers, though almost nowhere does he openly limn autobiographical details. Only those lovers of his work who have read, and read closely, lovingly, and intimately, all he has written, can understand the man. He is one of those authors of whom there can never be any biography away from his writings. . . . Though there are few so direct autobiographical indications as may be found in The Child of the House (essentially, and to some extent in actual detail, a record of the author's child-life), or as the statement in the Lamb essay that it was in a wood in the neighborhood of London that, as a child, he heard the cuckoo for the first time, the inner life of Walter Pater is written throughout each of his books, woven "like gold thread" through almost every page, though perhaps most closely and revealingly in Marius the Epicurean.[2]

1. *Letters*, ed. Evans, p. 59.
2. Sharp, "Some Personal Reminiscences of Walter Pater," *Atlantic Monthly* 74 (1894): 811.

In "The Child in the House," Pater's persona had set about to observe "some things in the story of his spirit—in that process of brain-building by which we are, each one of us, what we are" (*Miscellaneous Studies*, 173). By virtue of its vivid descriptions and nostalgic tone, this portrait seems inescapably a retrospective account in which Pater and his hero Florian share a common identity. We are told, for example, that it was "almost thirty years" (173) since Florian left his home when he was "about the age of twelve" (195). "The Child in the House" appeared in August of 1878 when Pater had just turned thirty-nine. If one takes into consideration the "almost" and the "about," there is a rather close resemblance in age. After "The Child in the House" and its incomplete sequel, "An English Poet," only *Marius* and the fragmentary *Gaston de Latour* can be said to display the *Künstlerroman* form of self-portraiture.

The curious thing about both "The Child in the House" and *Marius* is that each work was intended to be merely the first installment either in a continuing "series" or in a "trilogy" and that neither the contemplated series nor the trilogy was ever completed. On 17 April 1878, Pater wrote to George Grove, editor of *Macmillan's Magazine*: "I send you by this post a M.S. entitled *The House and the Child*, and should be pleased if you should like to have it for Macmillan's Magazine. It is not, as you may perhaps fancy, the first part of a work of fiction, but is meant to be complete in itself; though the first of a series, as I hope, with some real kind of sequence in them, and which I should be glad to send to *you*."[3] Arthur Symons reports that Pater told him "The Child in the House" was designed "to be the first chapter of a romance which was to show 'the poetry of modern life,' something, he said, as Aurora Leigh does."[4] Perhaps Symons

3. *Letters*, ed. Evans, pp. 29–30.
4. Symons, Introduction, *The Renaissance* (New York: Modern Library, [1919]), p. xxii.

misunderstood Pater's idea of a "series," or possibly Pater at some time did conceive of the piece as being "the first part of a work of fiction"; at any rate, the portrait appeared in *Macmillan's Magazine* entitled: "Imaginary Portraits. / I. The Child in the House." The superscription for the second installment read: "Imaginary Portraits / 2. An English Poet." Pater had begun working on this second portrait in 1878, and it may still have been in progress as late as 1881.[5] Its abrupt termination in midsentence suggests the loss, destruction, or cannibalizing of its final pages rather than the fragmentary trailing off of an unfinished work. It was posthumously printed in its unfinished state by May Ottley, a pupil of Pater's sister Clara, in the *Fortnightly Review*, 1 April 1931. Although Pater considered including the orphaned "Child in the House" in his 1887 collection of *Imaginary Portraits*, he chose to omit it because, as he wrote William Sharp on 23 May 1887, "I . . . found it would need many alterations, which I felt disinclined to make just then. I hope it may be included in some future similar series."[6] Symons recalled that as late as 1889 Pater "still spoke of finishing it," but "he was conscious that he could never continue it in the same style, and that it would not be satisfactory to rewrite it in his severer, later manner."[7] In 1894 Pater made minor alterations for a private printing of "The Child in the House" to be sold at a summer "fête" at which a performance of *Alice in Wonderland* was to be given in the Worcester College gardens—a charming grace note concluding what must have been, beneath, a self-lacerative failure.

Imagistic and thematic similarities between these two early portraits and *Marius the Epicurean* suggest that although Pater's initial autobiographical program was abandoned or (supposing a possible destruction of the concluding pages of

5. *Letters,* ed. Evans, pp. xxix, 35, 40; d'Hangest, *Pater,* 1: 366–67 n. 5.
6. *Letters,* ed. Evans, p. 72.
7. *Renaissance,* ed. Symons, p. xxii.

"An English Poet") suppressed much of its momentum was redirected into *Marius*—"an Imaginary Portrait of a peculiar type of mind in the time of Marcus Aurelius"[8]—and its unfinished companion, *Gaston de Latour*. In 1886 Pater wrote to an American correspondent that his first novel, *Marius*, was "designed to be the first of a kind of trilogy, or triplet, of works of a similar character; dealing with the same problems, under altered historical conditions. The period of the second of the series would be at the end of the 16th century, and the place France: of the third, the time, probably the end of the last century—and the scene, England."[9] *Marius* is dated 1881–84 and appeared in 1885. The first five chapters of Pater's unfinished second novel, *Gaston,* ran serially in *Macmillan's Magazine* from June to October 1888. Of the third novel, nothing exists except, perhaps, a few unpublished notes at Harvard's Houghton Library. As with his first projected series, Pater also found it impossible to relinquish plans for completion of his trilogy. As late as a year before his death, he seems to have been actively researching the historical background for *Gaston.* And if "The Child in the House" represented an embarrassing failure, Pater's second default in the same journal on so much greater a scale would have been felt as a catastrophe. Certainly Pater had canceled ideas for other series as well, as for example a collection of critical essays on Shakespeare, but what primarily distinguishes the plans for his autobiographical series is the failure of both the original and the alternate schemes, as well as his repeatedly voiced intentions of bringing them to completion. In order to explain *why* his second autobiographical project was still largely unfinished at his death in 1894, it is necessary to turn attention first to Pater's conception of criticism as "a second

8. *Letters,* ed. Evans, p. 52.
9. Ibid., p. 65.

and harder creation" (*Appreciations*, 126)—a creation of himself within the work of others—in order afterward to approach the psychological urgencies behind key passages of
self-revealing fantasy material.

For Pater the act of autobiography begins with a question
about his subjective or personal response to artistic presentation: "What is this song or picture, this engaging personality presented in life or in a book, to *me*? What effect does it
really produce on me? Does it give me pleasure? and if so,
what sort or degree of pleasure? How is my nature modified
by its presence, and under its influence?" (*Renaissance*, viii).
Describing the critical method of Charles Lamb, his closest
predecessor in the English tradition, Pater observes: "To feel
strongly the charm of an old poet or moralist, the literary
charm of Burton, for instance, or Quarles, or The Duchess of
Newcastle; and then to interpret that charm, to convey it to
others—he seeming to himself but to hand on to others, in
mere humble ministration, that of which for them he is really
the creator—this is the way of his criticism" (*Appreciations*,
112). Here Pater provides a formula for pulling together all his
varied writings—literary and art criticism, essays in the
history of myth, imaginary portraits—under the rubric of
criticism-as-creative-self-portraiture. On the one hand, Pater's nature is "modified" by the influence of the aesthetic
object he contemplates; on the other, by interpreting what he
feels, Pater modifies his readers' conceptions of the past and
creates his precursors anew in his own image. Employing,
like Lamb, an indirect means of self-revelation, Pater seldom
speaks in the first person in his portraits; and his reserve was
of so purposeful a nature as to cause Edmund Gosse, George
Moore, Arthur Symons, and Henry James to describe him as
wearing a "mask."[10] The distance Pater puts between him-

10. Gosse, *Critical Kit-Kats* (London: Heinemann, 1913), p. 266; Moore,
*Avowals* (New York: Boni and Liveright, 1919), p. 193; Symons, *Figures of*

self and the autobiographical masks used in his species of
narration is evidenced by the fact that, for the casual reader,
his writings have the appearance of impersonality. Yet it was
Pater himself who noted that Prosper Mérimée's "superb
self-effacement, his impersonality, is itself but an effective
personal trait" (*Miscellaneous Studies*, 37). Analyzing Lamb's
mode of autobiography masked by scholarly retrospection,
Pater writes that Lamb was

> essentially a scholar, and all his work mainly retro-
> spective; . . . his own sorrows, affections, perceptions,
> being alone real to him of the present. "I cannot make
> these present times," he says once, "present to me." . . .
> And with him, as with Montaigne, the desire of
> self-portraiture is, below all more superficial tenden-
> cies, the real motive in writing at all—a desire closely
> connected with that intimacy, that modern subjectiv-
> ity, which may be called the *Montaignesque* element in
> literature. What he designs is to give you himself, to
> acquaint you with his likeness; but must do this, if at
> all, indirectly, being indeed always more or less re-
> served, for himself and his friends. [*Appreciations*, 111,
> 117]

Given this clear emphasis upon criticism as a form of
creative self-portraiture, it is hardly surprising that Pater
should scorn (or at least remain indifferent to) the virtues of
verbatim transcription. In the history of Pater scholarship,
Pater's re-creative mistranscriptions were among the first
features of his style to receive extended comment. Samuel
Chew perceptively connected this "remarkable characteristic" of Pater's criticism "to the fundamental elements of his
temperament and manner of composition." Apart from "pas-

*Several Centuries* (London: Constable, 1916), p. 331 n. 1; James, *The Letters of Henry James*, ed. Percy Lubbock (New York: Scribner's, 1920), 1: 222.

sages that are confessedly centos of phrases," Pater's use of
quotations (translations as well as quotations from English
sources) is characterized by "the separation of passages
joined in the original, the junction of passages far distant in
the original, unnoted omissions, and, in some cases, mis-
translations. This does not imply dishonest or careless work;
it is intentional, yet with no thought of deception, being
closely related as a literary device to Pater's whole manner of
composition." Though he recognizes Pater's creative misquotation as a "literary device," Chew remains content simply to inquire: "has the critic a right to do this?"[11] Very much
the same question was asked by Christopher Ricks more
than sixty years later: "What if 'faith to one's own meaning'
can be achieved only by faithlessness to another's meaning?
. . . Pater's rights leave little room for anyone else's or anything else's."[12] Ricks, seemingly unaware of previous dis-
cussions of this topic, reopens the question by attacking
Pater: "As someone who believes that Arnold's little finger is
worth Pater's whole hand of little fingers, I regret its not
simply being the case that Arnold's modest shrewdness
about the function of criticism leads him to quote impecca-
bly, while Pater's quasi-creative arrogation misleads him to
misquote peccably." Ricks observes that Harold Bloom
"glories in the claim that Pater's 'writings obscure the supposed distinction between criticism and creation' " and in
rebuttal quotes Arnold to the effect that everyone " 'would
be willing to admit as a general proposition, that the critical
faculty is lower than the inventive.' " Yet in an 1863 letter to
Sainte-Beuve reassuring him of the genuine artistry of his

11. Chew, "Pater's Quotations," *Nation* 99 (1914): 404. See also Helen
Law, "Pater's Use of Greek Quotations," *Modern Language Notes* 58 (1943):
575–85.
    12. Ricks, "Pater, Arnold and Misquotation," *Times Literary Supplement*,
25 November 1977, p. 1384, cols. 3, 5.

sort of criticism, Arnold himself had inquired rhetorically if being remembered as a critic rather than as a poet was "a cause for complaint? I think not. Great critics (and you are one of them) have always been rarer than great poets." And after Sainte-Beuve's death, Arnold wrote that he was unwilling to accept Sainte-Beuve's estimate that at best his essays were "judicious things in a second-rate genre." Although Sainte-Beuve would not rank with Milton, said Arnold, "first-rate criticism has a permanent value higher than that of any but first-rate poetry and art."[13]

What Ricks lacks is a certain perspective on the function of criticism which would allow him to accept "the creation of something personal to the critic": "Pater's misquotations," he nonetheless rightly points out, "are the rewriting of his authors so that they say special Paterian things. Arnold's misquotations . . . are the rewriting of his authors so that they say unspecial things." To illustrate, Ricks observes that Pater's preference for "finer" over "fine" or "finest" leads him to a "creative substitution"; for, "unlike the comparative, the superlative implies a climax, a completion, an outcome, rather than an endless process and 'a tension of nerve.' " Hence, Shakespeare's "fine issues" becomes for Pater a comparative: "In *Measure for Measure,* as in some other of his plays, Shakespeare has remodelled an earlier and somewhat rough composition to 'finer issues,' . . . 'has refashioned . . . materials already at hand, so that the relics of other men's poetry are incorporated.' " Ricks comments:

> The rough had become the fine; the fine is now to become the finer. Literature, as Pater often (and sometimes italicizedly) says, is the *"fine* art"; criticism has

13. "Sainte-Beuve," *The Complete Prose Works of Matthew Arnold,* ed. R. H. Super (Ann Arbor: University of Michigan Press, 1965), 5: 305–06, quoted in Richard M. Chadbourne, *Charles-Augustin Sainte-Beuve* (Boston, G. K. Hall, 1977), p. 172.

then to be the finer art. Hence such a spiral as this: "It is a finer ideal, extracted from what in relation to any actual world is already an ideal. Like some strange second flowering after date, it renews on a more delicate type the poetry of a past age, but must not be confounded with it." Pater is speaking of an artistic movement, "Aesthetic Poetry," but he is contemplating too his own criticism—or, to him, criticism. Criticism too is a strange second flowering, a renewing on a more delicate type of the poetry of a past age.

Given his perception of Pater's purpose, it is curious that Ricks should cite a line from the Leonardo essay—"No one ever ruled over the mere *subject* in hand more entirely than Leonardo, or bent it more dexterously to purely artistic ends"—and stubbornly insist: "But if your subject is Leonardo's art"—if, that is, you are not an artist but merely a critic writing about an artist—"the case is altered." But, of course, since Pater conceives of himself as being in every sense as committed an artist as Leonardo, the case certainly is *not* altered. If, in Lisa, Leonardo could pursue his vision of the ideal lady, Pater can pursue his personal vision in Leonardo's work; and it is for this reason that he deconstructs the elements of Leonardo's art in order to weave them anew according to his own inner feelings.[14]

In this search for himself in others, Pater's debt to Sainte-Beuve is a larger one than to Lamb. "Criticism is for me a metamorphosis," wrote Sainte-Beuve, "I try to disappear in the character I am reproducing." Or again, "If I had to judge myself, pursuing self-love in all its disguises, I would say: 'S-B. paints no portrait without reflecting himself in it;

14. Ricks, "Misquotation," p. 1383, cols. 1, 2; p. 1384, col. 5; p. 1385, cols. 1, 2.

18 CRITICISM AS CREATION

on the pretext of depicting someone else, it is always his own profile which he describes.' "[15] Like Pater, Sainte-Beuve had begun as an unsuccessful lyric poet but found a more congenial mode of self-portraiture in the indirect revelation of the *Portraits littéraires* and *Portraits contemporains*. Both Sainte-Beuve and Pater convert their presence into an integral part of the portrait by dramatizing their quest for the distinctive talent or psychological formula of the biographical subject in their style, subject choice, arrangement or omission of facts, selection of extended excerpts, and manipulation of sources. Generally, Sainte-Beuve's sketches open with a leisurely preamble, abruptly terminated by the introduction of biographical data, such as dates, which then modulate into a loose assemblage of juxtaposed facts and fancy, detail and generalization. Sainte-Beuve also frequently "re-invents" neglected secondary figures as if they were purely imaginary characters, focusing on those distinctive clues in their early creations which reveal future development. Not only in all of this do Pater's early essays seem indebted to the French critic, but they also share with Sainte-Beuve's work a sense of flux that implies the absence of a central or continuous self either in the author, in his biographical subject, or in his readers. "Every day I change," wrote Sainte-Beuve: "Before the final death of this mobile being who calls himself by my name, how many men have already died within me? You think I speak only of myself, reader; but ponder a moment and see if this does not also apply to you." With this passage in mind, Richard Chadbourne, Sainte-Beuve's best scholar, writes: "At times, like Montaigne and Pascal, Sainte-Beuve was skeptical that any such underlying 'fond solide' existed beneath the fluctuating phenomena ('l'ondoyant') of human

15. Quoted in Chadbourne, *Sainte-Beuve*, pp. 104, 103. Pater frequently cites Sainte-Beuve, most notably in *The Renaissance* and the Postscript to *Appreciations*.

nature. 'Who can say the final word of others? Do we even
know it of ourselves?' he asked. Do we possess true sub-
stance ('un fond véritable') or are we merely 'unending surfaces' ('des surfaces à l'infini')? Yet in the same context he
makes it clear that he is prepared, despite his skepticism, to
persist in search of this fleeting reality."[16]

Pater's skepticism as to a centrality or continuity or fixed
origin of identity within quotidian experience reflected not
only the Gallic tradition of Sainte-Beuve and his predecessors, Montaigne and Pascal, but also recent British scientific
thought: T. H. Huxley, Charles Darwin, Charles Lyell,
J. F. W. Herschel, and Robert Chambers, whose covert or
direct materialism, although sometimes qualifying with de-
velopmental references the vision of nature red in tooth and
claw, represented a disturbing challenge to Oxford notions of
fixed principles. In the opening paragraphs of the Conclusion to *The Renaissance*, Pater questioned man's sense of
fixed identity by describing his fundamental oneness with
the perpetual flux—the human body as the confluence of
random physical forces soon parting and the psyche as a web
of impressions continually weaving and unweaving. The individual seems merely a centripetal converging of elements
scattered by the centrifugal thrust of the flux; his circle of self
has no definite boundary that endures through time; moment
by moment he changes. Identity, temporalized in this fashion, consists in a succession of selves, each of which merely
contains a "relic" of the self that preceded it. And as with
man's body and psyche, so also with the "original products
of human genius." Thus, even Plato himself was at an infinite remove from the sources of western higher culture:

Some of the results of patient earlier thinkers, even
then dead and gone, are of the structure of his philos-

16. Ibid., p. 98.

ophy. They are everywhere in it, not as the stray
carved corner of some older edifice, to be found here
or there amid the new, but rather like minute relics of
earlier organic life in the very stone he builds with. . . .
The thoughts of Plato, like the language he has to use
(we find it so again, in turn, with those predecessors
of his, when we pass from him to them) are covered
with the traces of previous labour and have had their
earlier proprietors. . . . In Plato, in spite of his wonderful savour of literary freshness, there is nothing ab-
solutely new: or rather, as in many other very original
products of human genius, the seemingly new is old
also, a palimpsest, a tapestry of which the actual
threads have served before, or like the animal frame
itself, every particle of which has already lived and died
many times over. [*Plato*, 7–8]

Pater here formulates out of contemporary philosophic and
scientific concepts the notion that consciousness and language are grounded in an unending regression of "relics"
and "traces."

Some years before Pater, Edward FitzGerald and Dante
Gabriel Rossetti had pioneered translation as an art form
(later developed in Ezra Pound's work) by "reinterpreting" a
Persian philosopher and the early Italian poets. Partially pro-
tected by the persona of the original author, they produced a
poetry liberated from assumptions implicit in the literature
of Queen Victoria's age. But the reason Pater had his heroes
encounter in their first fluid form the literary works of their
eras as they came into being is not that he needed the freedom to flout nineteenth-century conventions, nor did he
need freedom from, in Stanley Fish's phrase, the "lexico-
graphic lockstep" of the schoolboy's faithful crib; rather, he
wanted to dramatize the process of dissolving one con-

sciousness in the self-expression of another, of appropriating or annexing at first hand the fluid content of other minds and fathering anew their compositions. For insofar as all things are in perpetual flux, literature, too, will be in need of perpetual renewal, generation to generation. Assessing Pascal's debt to Montaigne, Pater says: "one of the leading interests in the study of Pascal is to trace the influence upon him of the typical sceptic of the preceding century. Pascal's 'Thoughts' we shall never understand unless we realise the undertexture in them of Montaigne's very phrases. . . . Pascal reechoes Montaigne then in asserting the paradoxical character of man and his experience" (*Miscellaneous Studies,* 84). As in the reechoing of Montaigne by Pascal (who is re-reechoed by Sainte-Beuve, who again is re-re-reechoed by Pater), so too, for example, Pater's remastering or reenacting of Leonardo's portrait of the Mona Lisa in *The Renaissance,* deliberately dissolving a historically existing work in his own imaginatively re-created text, is meant to display a repetition which is part of an endless chain of assimilation. Writing of Plato's thought, Pater observes: "Nothing but the life-giving principle of cohesion is new; the new perspective, the resultant complexion, and expressiveness which familiar thoughts attain by novel juxtaposition. In other words, the *form* is new. But then, in the creation of philosophical literature, as in all other products of art, *form,* in the full signification of that word, is everything, and the mere matter is nothing" (*Plato,* 8). This dissolving of an original subject into echoing and reechoing forms is emphatically present in the work of the artists of the Renaissance—in Giorgione, who is reflected more in the work of others than seen in his own right, or in Leonardo, the number of whose "authentic works is very small indeed" but who is seen through "a multitude of other men's pictures. . . . Sometimes . . . we have a hand, rough enough by contrast, working upon some fine hint or sketch

of his. Sometimes . . . the lost originals have been re-echoed
and varied upon again and again. . . . At other times the
original remains, but has been a mere theme or motive, a type
of which the accessories might be modified or changed; and
these variations have but brought out the more the purpose,
or expression of the original" (*Renaissance*, 117–18).

If originality is but an echoing with modifications, it is
equally true that even a frank echoing is a kind of original
creation with "variations" personal to the copyist. Style, says
Pater in his essay on Raphael, is a matter of selection and
assertion of oneself. When Raphael stood before a picture to
copy it,

> and so copying, quite unconsciously, and with no
> disloyalty to his original, refined, improved, sub-
> stituted,—substituted himself, in fact, his finer
> self—he had already struck the persistent note of his
> career. . . . He will realise the function of style as
> exemplified in the practice of Da Vinci, face to face
> with the world of nature and man as they are; select-
> ing from, asserting one's self in a transcript of its ver-
> itable *data*; like drawing to like there, in obedience
> to the master's preference for the embodiment of
> the creative form within him. [*Miscellaneous Studies*,
> 40, 50]

Pater ascribes to Sandro Botticelli also just this sort of
transcription which surpasses the objective givens of experience in order to expound "visions of its own." He writes:
"Giotto, the tried companion of Dante, Masaccio, Ghirlan-
dajo even, do but transcribe, with more or less refining, the
outward image; they are dramatic, not visionary painters;
they are almost impassive spectators of the action before
them. But the genius of which Botticelli is the type usurps
the data before it as the exponent of ideas, moods, visions of

its own; in this interest it plays fast and loose with those data, rejecting some and isolating others, and always combining them anew" (*Renaissance*, 53–54). Isolating and combining anew the facts of his experience, Botticelli succeeds in identifying outward reality as no longer extrinsic to the self but as that in which his own visions consist.

In "Style," Pater cites this visionary approach as the essence of any artistic prose expression:

> Your historian, for instance, with absolutely truthful intention, amid the multitude of facts presented to him must needs select, and in selecting assert something of his own humour, something that comes not of the world without but of a vision within. So Gibbon . . . Livy, Tacitus, Michelet . . . each, after his own sense, modifies—who can tell where and to what degree?— and becomes something else than a transcriber; each, as he thus modifies, passing into the domain of art proper. For just in proportion as the writer's aim, consciously or unconsciously, comes to be the transcribing, not of the world, not of mere fact, but of his sense of it, he becomes an artist, his work *fine* art. . . . And further, all beauty is in the long run only *fineness* of truth, or what we call expression, the finer accommodation of speech to that vision within. [*Appreciations*, 9–10]

Thus, in this same essay on style, for example, Pater links into a single block paragraph extracts from several letters to different correspondents, as if Flaubert's letters to Maxime Du Camp, Alfred Le Poittevin, and Ernest Chevalier were a single missive addressed to Louise Colet. Or earlier, in his essay on Michelangelo, preferring stimulating readings to textually accurate ones, Pater freely chose his quotations from the corrupt 1623 edition of the poems as well as from the authoritative version established by Cesare Guasti. Indeed, at one point in the essay Pater cited a line from the corrupt text of Michelangelo's grandnephew and a second line, apparently, from the text of Guasti but then altered, without even the authority of the grandnephew, Guasti's *foco* to *raggio* (*Renaissance*, 84). And in *Marius*, to cite a final example, among the translations and paraphrases from Aurelius's *Meditations*, arranged out of all sequence with respect to the historical document he is quoting, Pater has the emperor using, not quite accurately, the words of Prospero's famous speech in *The Tempest*—"We are such stuff as dreams are made of" (*Marius*, 1: 204)—and echoing a half line from Pope's *Essay on Man*—"Whatever is, is right" (2: 52).

Such modifications of sources occur because Pater's subjects are Pater himself. As the specific details of action and scene dissolve themselves into moments recollected across the distance of time, the consciousnesses of author and character become inextricably interwoven. Although startling, it is necessary to insist that like Pythagoras of *Plato and Platonism* or the Mona Lisa of *The Renaissance*, whose consciousness spans the centuries and epitomizes history in a culminating vision of the present moment, Pater envisions himself also as a figure of multiple selfhood. In this, Pater's art of autobiography assumes the personality to be a web of cultural relationships and the individual to be the visible image of an infinite companionship of like-oriented selves that pervade and shape the personality. Describing the "perpetual weaving and unweaving of ourselves" (*Renaissance*, 236) in the Conclusion to *The Renaissance*, Pater depicted identity as a fantastically complex palimpsest of physical and cultural threads. Pater's typical hero is an almost incorporeal presence whose personality is covertly implied and whose physical existence seems to inhere in the "texts" of his age, a living text as it were, woven from the aesthetic artifacts—

poetry, prose, painting, sculpture, architecture—of the past. Just as the Mona Lisa or the Dionysus of *Greek Studies* had represented for Pater a condensing of the flux of experience and history into a single sensible image, so the aesthetic hero is simply Pater as Pater's converging threads of identity existed in cultural artifacts a hundred or many hundreds of years previously (and as Pater's text ultimately becomes an Ur-version of his reader as many years later).

In this process of pursuing a reflection of himself in other men's work, Pater clearly strives for a double perspective which refuses to assign pride of place either to the original or to its reflection. Is the other text the original and Pater's merely a reflection of it, or is Pater's version the original and the earlier text now but a prevenient phantom? Thus, in *Marius,* the fixed literary works of antiquity, the writings of Apuleius, Fronto, Aurelius, and Lucian, are pushed back to the moment of formulation, of preinscription, and by a curious warp of chronology an ab-original cento of their contents is woven for the Victorian reader. In "Sebastian van Storck" Pater had done much the same thing with Spinoza's *Ethics,* and in *Gaston* the preexisting texts of Montaigne and, less directly, of Ronsard, Bruno, and Brantôme are returned to their first fluid form. A danger here is that in the repetition force, incisiveness, and heat can give way to what is "fainter and more spectral."[17] Of Bruno, Pater writes: "It was *intimate* discourse; . . . the sort of speech which, consolidated into literary form as a book, would be a dialogue according to the true Attic genius. . . . What Gaston then heard was, in truth, the first fervid expression of all those contending views out of which his written works would afterwards be compacted, of course with much loss of heat in the process" (*Gaston,* 155, 157). Bruno's "loss of heat" in the act of repeating himself is present to an even greater degree in the corrupt text of

17. Pater, "Poems by William Morris," p. 300.

Michelangelo's grandnephew: "He omitted much, re-wrote
the sonnets in part, and sometimes compressed two or more
compositions into one, always losing something of the force
and incisiveness of the original" (*Renaissance*, 82–83). So,
too, the disciples of Giorgione and Leonardo echo their
masters at one remove from the passionate and powerful
originals; also the corpselike art of Fra Angelico, as Pater described it in the essay on Winckelmann, with its exaggerated
inwardness from which the sensuous elements have escaped is in need of being returned to the Hellenic sources of
color and design "to be clarified and corrected" (199). Only a
true artist—Raphael, Botticelli, Leonardo, Plato, or, certainly,
Sainte-Beuve or Pater—can repeat the past without loss of
force, incisiveness, or heat, because only the true artist has
the vision to recombine old material in powerfully novel
ways.

In the search for a form in which the past most effectively
can be repeated with no loss of personal force, Pater created
the imaginary portrait. One might trace a gamut from the
unmelodious and abstract prose of "Diaphanéité" and
"Coleridge's Writings" to those overdetermined passages of
unconscious fantasy in the *Renaissance* essays on Botticelli
and Leonardo, passages which outwardly still retain the
semblance of criticism. In the 1878 "Child in the House,"
Pater created his first true imaginary portrait: "Imaginary—
and portraits, they present, not an action, a story: but a
character—personality, revealed, especially, in outward detail."[18] Yet even these imaginary portraits remain what Edmund Gosse called "essays in criticism by fiction";[19] and,
were the first word in Pater's description not "imaginary" but
"critical," he would have been offering here a description of
his *Renaissance* essays. Pater's work crosses the line (if a line

18. Quoted in d'Hangest, *Pater*, 2: 356 n. 11.
19. Gosse, "Mr. Walter Pater on Platonism," *New Review* 8 (1893): 421.

can be drawn) between critical and imaginary portraiture in his review of Octave Feuillet's novel, *La morte*, written, significantly, at the same time (1886) as the four works collected in *Imaginary Portraits*. Though the pretext of a review keeps "Feuillet's *'La Morte'*" closer to its critical origins than, say, "Hippolytus Veiled," the generic similarity of Feuillet's novel to Pater's other imaginary portraits separates this review from the other essays in *Appreciations* where, to the dismay of every reader since 1890, it had been placed in the second edition as a substitute for the suppressed "Aesthetic Poetry."

That there is no difference in kind between critical and imaginary portraits is suggested by the minute gradations that separate (or relate, rather) what Pater considers a work of criticism, his review of Feuillet's novel, and a work he himself labeled an imaginary portrait, "Hippolytus Veiled," subtitled "A Study from Euripides." In "Feuillet's *'La Morte,'*" Pater radically abridges and translates portions of the French novel in order to transform it into an English short story of sorts; in "Hippolytus Veiled," he reconstructs, with the help of Seneca and Ovid, Euripides's lost drama. "Hippolytus" clearly is separated by only a small step from "A Prince of Court Painters" collected in the *Imaginary Portraits* volume. Although in this study of Watteau's career Pater attributes to the characters imaginary relationships, the figures themselves are all historically real; moreover, Pater's strategy of "Extracts from an Old French Journal" parallels his method with Feuillet: extracts from an obscure French novel. Though other imaginary portraits lie at greater distances from criticism, even in *Marius* only its hero is wholly Pater's invention, and most of its other events and characters are taken from actual sources and fulfill a critical function. Undoubtedly, the attraction of the imaginary lay for Pater in the greater scope it afforded for self-exploration and self-

portraiture. Possibly also the charges of inaccuracy leveled
against *The Renaissance* by Mrs. Mark Pattison and others led
Pater away from the fixed subject matter of criticism. But the
increased freedom of the imaginary mode also heightened
the threat of self-exposure and misunderstanding. Ultimately, for this reason *Plato and Platonism*, Pater's most impersonal work competed with and overwhelmed the personal
issues under exploration in his autobiographical trilogy.

If Pater's search for that reflection of himself in others is
constituted less by action, story, or events than by character
or personality, how well can that Other be known, given the
fact that consciousness and language are grounded in an infinite regression of "relics" and "traces"? In his early essay,
"Aesthetic Poetry," Pater wrote:

> The composite experience of all the ages is part of each
> one of us; to deduct from that experience, to obliterate
> any part of it, to come face to face with the people of a
> past age, as if the middle age, the Renaissance, the
> eighteenth century had not been, is as impossible as
> to become a little child, or enter again into the womb
> and be born. But though it is not possible to repress a
> single phase of that humanity, which, because we live
> and move and have our being in the life of humanity,
> makes us what we are; it is possible to isolate such a
> phase, to throw it into relief, to be divided against
> ourselves in zeal for it, as we may hark back to some
> choice space of our own individual life. We cannot
> conceive the age; we can conceive the element it has
> contributed to our culture; we can treat the subjects of
> the age bringing that into relief, . . . aspiring to but
> never actually reaching its way of conceiving life.[20]

20. Pater, "Poems by William Morris," p. 307.

Granted that one is able to "isolate," "throw into relief," "be divided against" oneself, and "hark back to" certain periods of time—either personal or cultural—one cannot, says Pater, "deduct," "obliterate," or "repress" one's personal or cultural experience. There is, Pater says, playing on biblical statements by Nicodemus and the apostle Paul, no getting back to absolute origins, no return to beginnings, only "an aspiring to" but never an actual reaching of the essential past. There is, then, no knowledge of others apart from the subjectivities of one's own perceptions, cultural and personal. But although Pater's life never can coincide with past experience, neither are the lives in the past essentially other; specifically they are, as a division of self against self, his doppelgänger. In this, Pater's relation to figures in the historical past appears most akin to that "finer sort of memory" (*Miscellaneous Studies*, 172) that colors the childhood recollections of Florian Deleal or akin to Marius's return to a "choice space" in his personal experience that takes the form of an idealized and selective reminiscence: "he lived much, and as it were by system, in reminiscence. . . . Detached from him, yet very real, there lay certain spaces of his life, in delicate perspective, under a favourable light; and, somehow, all the less fortunate detail and circumstance had parted from them" (*Marius*, 1: 154). Just as one's childhood or youth is idealized by memory yet remains an accessible part of oneself, so also that alter ego from the past—that self which lives implicatively within the literary and artistic "texts" of its age—is understood to be part of the author's present being.

When the past inheres harmoniously in the present "in delicate perspective," the doppelgänger is complementary; but when the ideal symmetry is disrupted, there is a fragmentation of harmony and a conflict of self against self. This harmony is not only an access to time past; it can be an approach to any unified ground of consciousness, to any elusive Other. In Marius's mystical experience at the inn located in the Sabine hills, Pater describes his hero's sense of the double: "Through a dreamy land he could see himself moving, as if in another life, and like another person, through all his fortunes and misfortunes, passing from point to point, weeping, delighted, escaping from various dangers" (2: 66). As Marius withdraws ever deeper into his reverie, the sense of identity with his double, now become a suprapersonal companion, provides an expanded consciousness of selfhood beyond the range of his personal experience: "It was as if there were not one only, but two wayfarers, side by side, visible there across the plain, . . . and . . . he passed from that mere fantasy of a self not himself, beside him in his coming and going, to those divinations of a living and companionable spirit at work in all things" (2: 67–68). As here, unity with the double is the ideal; but because the childhood world of innocence is subject to a kind of Blakean fall or loss of wholeness, a false contrast or antagonism appears as the self matures, the ideal of a perfect love is lost, and the disembodied dreams of the soul become delirium. Coleridge the "narcotist" is a prime example of a self split into conflicting halves: "he is the victim of a division of the will, often showing itself in trivial things: he could never choose on which side of the garden path he would walk. . . . Coleridge, by what he did, what he was, and what he failed to do, represents that inexhaustible discontent, languor, and homesickness, the chords of which ring all through our modern literature."[21]

This failure to find a reflection of oneself in the Other, a failure dramatized by some form of division, expressed itself in Pater's own life as it had in Coleridge's. Pater writes, describing Charles and Mary Lamb but perhaps thinking of

21. Pater, "Coleridge's Writings," *Westminster Review* NS 29 (1866): 117, 132.

himself and the more intellectual of his sisters, Clara: "Jack and Jill sitting thus side by side, till one sat alone in the faint sun at last, in a way, the anticipation of which sounds sometimes as a too poignant note in the sweetly-linked music of their intercourse."[22] Or again, in the conflict of impulse and restraint in the lives of his King's School contemporaries, Pater noted, so Thomas Wright affirms, the way his schoolmates had "of reproducing, unsuspectingly, the humours of animal nature. . . . Throughout the sprightly movement of the lads' daily life it was as if their 'tribal' pets or monsters were with or within them. Tall Exmes, lithe and cruel like a tiger—it was pleasant to stroke him. The tiger was there, the parrot, the hare, the goat of course, and certainly much apishness" (*Gaston*, 34).[23] Later, in the essay on Mérimée, Pater inquires: "Were there not survivals of the old wild creatures in the gentlest, the politest of us?" (*Miscellaneous Studies*, 28); and, after commenting on Mérimée's artistic elaboration of this idea, Pater then compares Mérimée himself to a serpent. Pater rather tongue-in-cheek revealed his own totem at a luncheon party at which the question was raised among the guests: " 'What creature would one like to be, if not a man?' When Pater's turn came, he said, 'A carp.' He pictured himself immemorially swimming in the green waters of some royal château."[24] In Pater's writings variations on this pattern of division—grounded, as I shall argue later, in his early familial experience—are pervasive: Amis and Amile, Winckelmann and Goethe, Marius and Cornelius, Watteau and Marie-Marguerite, Duke Carl and Gretchen, Aliette and Bernard, James and Emerald, Hip-

22. Pater, "The Character of the Humourist: Charles Lamb," *Fortnightly Review*, NS 24 (1878): 473.

23. Wright, *The Life of Walter Pater* (London: Everett, 1907), 1: 97.

24. D. S. MacColl, "A Batch of Memories: XII—Walter Pater," *Week-end Review*, 12 December 1931, p. 760.

polytus and Antiope, Hyacinth and Prior Saint-Jean, Columbe and Gaston, even Socrates and Plato. The common pattern is the absence or death of the one and the grief of the other, initiating by this splitting apart into opposed states a fall from innocence and a quest to regain that lost ideal of harmony.

The world of art offers itself as the way to harmonize the contrasting phases of the doppelgänger by its power to transfigure or idealize the human condition. In the 1866 Morris review, Pater said that "Greek poetry, mediaeval or modern poetry, projects above the realities of its time a world in which the forms of things are transfigured."[25] And shortly thereafter Pater remarked in "Winckelmann": "The basis of all artistic genius lies in the power of conceiving humanity in a new and striking way, of putting a happy world of its own creation in place of the meaner world of our common days, generating around itself an atmosphere with a novel power of refraction, selecting, transforming, recombining the images it transmits, according to the choice of the imaginative intellect" (Renaissance, 213–14). Indeed, the life-restoring harmony of art effects a progressive idealization of life from generation to generation. Pater's hero Gaston discovers, for example, on his visit to "Le cabinet des peintures du roi" that the beholder, rapt "in the admiration of visible beauty," will cause that ideal to exist again,

> renewing the world, handing on, as a pledge of love
> and kindness for ever, the beauty which had kindled
> it, the likeness of, or an improvement upon itself,
> kindling a like love in turn, linking paternally, filially,
> age to age, the young to the old, marriage, mater-
> nity, childhood and youth, consecrated by indefeasi-
> ble union with the [?Creator], who looks favourably

25. Pater, "Poems by William Morris," p. 300.

also on the virginity, the restraint which in fact se-
cures the purity, the ardency therefore, of the creative flame: this was what Gaston found in . . . those
mature Italian masters. . . . Here art, according to
its proper ministry, had been at once an interpretation and an idealisation of life.[26]

Given the unexpected or incongruous tragedies which con-
clude Pater's portraits, it might seem inconsistent to speak of
the ideality of the world of art. However, the idealization of
life by art is conceived by Pater as the conquest and reconciliation, or at least as the organization and constitution of
continuity between, the antinomies of life and death, beauty
and horror, the real and the imaginary, and not as the exclu-
sion or isolation of the one condition from the other.

The dramatization in Pater's writings of this continuity
between antinomies is based upon a pattern common to a
variety of myths which Pater employs. As Marius reenacts
the Cupid-Psyche story, for example, so Gaston and Columbe reenact the Zeus-Semele myth. When the godhead,
Cupid or Zeus, is withdrawn, the mortal, Psyche or Semele,
suffers a loss of wholeness. Semele, like Psyche, "desires to
see her lover. . . . But the mortal may not behold him and
live. Semele gives premature birth to the child Dionysus,"
and her "death in childbirth" makes him "a seven months'
child, cast out among its enemies, motherless" (*Greek
Studies*, 24–25). Marius without his counterpart and Gaston
and Columbe without each other correspond to Psyche and
Semele after their loss of Cupid and Zeus. Three archetypes
for the oscillation between complementary and antagonistic
phases are primary: Dionysus in his summer and winter as-
pects; the contrasting phases of life and death, innocence and
corruption, embodied in Demeter's two daughters, Kore and

26. Quoted in d'Hangest, *Pater*, 2: 365 n. 19.

Persephone; and the myth of Polydeuces and Castor (43–44;
*Plato*, 230–31). This last, the myth of the Dioscuri, tells of the
twin stars Gemini, "those two half-earthly, half-celestial
brothers, one of whom, Polydeuces, was immortal. The
other, Castor, the younger, subject to old age and death, had
fallen in battle, was found breathing his last. Polydeuces
thereupon, at his own prayer, was permitted to die: with un-
dying fraternal affection, had foregone one moiety of his
privilege, and lay in the grave for a day in his brother's stead,
but shone out again on the morrow; the brothers thus ever
coming and going, interchangeably, but both alike gifted
now with immortal youth."

An analogous, reciprocal interplay between opposites is
perceived by Pater in the sphere of the arts generally: "although each art has . . . its own specific order of impressions,
and an untranslatable charm, while a just apprehension of
the ultimate differences of the arts is the beginning of aesthetic criticism; yet it is noticeable that, in its special mode of
handling its given material, each art may be observed to pass
into the condition of some other art, by what German critics
term as *Anders-streben*—a partial alienation from its own
limitations, through which the arts are able, not indeed to
supply the place of each other, but reciprocally to lend each
other new forces" (*Renaissance*, 133–34). Although there are
"untranslatable" "ultimate differences," yet each passes into
the condition of the other by transcending its limitations and
"reciprocally" lending the other new force. If the arts are not
precisely able "to supply the place of each other," the relation of the visionary soul to the house in which it lives
actually seems to obliterate or, at least, reconcile all distinctions: "For such an orderly soul, as life proceeds, all sorts
of delicate affinities establish themselves, between herself
and the doors and passage-ways, the lights and shadows, of
her outward dwelling-place, until she may seem incorporate
with it—until at last, in the entire expressiveness of what is

outward, there is for her, to speak properly, between outward and inward, no longer any distinction at all" (*Marius*, 2: 93). Earlier, in "The Child in the House," Pater's alter ego, Florian, meditated on the interrelation of the child and its house: "inward and outward being woven through and through each other into one inextricable texture" (*Miscellaneous Studies*, 173).

The continuity between antinomies found in the relation of one art form to another or in the relation of the soul to its house has its ultimate expression in the basic differential relationship of the mythic double. What is important for Pater in the relation of the summer to the winter Dionysus, of Kore to Persephone, or of Polydeuces to Castor is that they are mutually creator and created and that neither figure in the mythic equation has a ground of being apart from his interplay with the other, for each, as a creation of alterity, is constituted reciprocally. Speaking in *Plato* of the ontological extremes of pure being over against concrete phenomena, Pater observed that "at both ends of experience there is —nothing!" (*Plato*, 35). This absence of "being" apart from a relational interplay is dramatically embodied in the myths of the doppelgänger and becomes for Pater the key to understanding the relation between inner and outer textual levels, illustrative of the relation of the author to his narrative, of the narrative to its literary antecedents, and of the reader to the text and its author. No single level constitutes the "ground-situation" or can exist apart from a ceaseless deconstructing-reconstructing interplay of the plot and its regressing inner levels of antecedents with the next frame out, the authorial level of composition, and its expanding series of frames beyond as the text is read and assimilated. Neither the author's life nor the story of his hero constitutes a self-contained unit or achieves any meaning apart from the other; neither is the origin of the other or that to which the one can be referred as the explanation of the other. The hero is thus bound to fail to

capture "wholeness" or "being" adequately because within
the scope of the plot "wholeness" or "being" manifests itself
as absence; so, too, the author apart from his compositional
role finds within his own quotidian existence an appalling
lack of continuity and pattern—only a series of discontinu-
ous selves, as the Conclusion to *The Renaissance* describes
identity.

But in the dialectic between the autobiographer shaping
his life and the emergent work which reflects and enhances
that identity, a new kind of unity is revealed. Pater's im-
potence in life (his almost melodramatically sequestered
existence, as when staying at a hotel he would leave if spoken to) and his heroes' passivity (as in Marius's failure to
achieve a heroic martyrdom)—these curiously unresolved
existences find fulfillment in each other. The attempt to capture or fix that coherent center of self is abandoned for a
center within the interplay of author and narrative, a center
always in movement away from the present toward layers
deeper within or frames further outside. Yet, undeniably,
the diachronic alternation of the antagonistic doppelgänger,
each half of which contains within it only an indirect trace of
its opposite, is stabilized "in delicate perspective" on the
synchronic canvas of the text. This interwoven or reflexive
quality, this turning back on itself of a writing that refuses to
step aside, to become invisible, and to re-present directly a
life or set of occurrences, clearly moves artistic self-consciousness to the foreground, calls attention to the work's
fictiveness, and insists upon textual inscription as the only
place wherein the simulacra of the inner and outer levels of
experience—parallel, concentric, coinherent—are reified. As
the immortal Polydeuces dies in Castor's stead, so each level
of the text is dissolved in the other in order to shine out again
recomposed—author and critic coming and going interchangeably throughout history.

# CHAPTER TWO

# Visionary Texts

Unlike a painting, projected spatially and perceived simultaneously, the literary work, apprehended sequentially, is deeply rooted in time. But in his essay, "Style," Pater seems to subvert Lessing's distinction: "As the painter in his picture, so the artist in his book, aims at the production by honourable artifice of a peculiar atmosphere" (*Appreciations*, 18). Although generated by temporality and flux, Pater's art perversely aspires, syntactically, to the atmosphere of a painting or a tapestry: static, pictorial, nonlinear. His complicated syntax, threatening always to break the cognitive sequence, resembles the highly inflected structure of the classical languages, which permits a more arbitrary order of words so that the sentence seems to present to the reader all of its parts simultaneously. Within Pater's sentences, there are few stressed terms but a host of differential relationships masking a core idea so deeply embedded or splintered among qualifications and nonstructural appendages that readers, lost among Pater's involutions and ambiguities, have damned his style as lifeless and artificial. But by moving authorial self-consciousness to the foreground, Pater's text intentionally prohibits that willing suspension of disbelief by which conventional fiction, spontaneously stepping aside and becoming invisible, conveys experience directly to the reader. Instead, Pater's prose affirms its artifice in order to approach, through a self-sustaining imaginative structure, that elusive unity which is always escaping. Pater's achievement in the three volumes written prior to his creative crisis of 1888—*Studies in the History of the Renaissance* (1873), *Marius the Epicurean* (1885), and *Imaginary Portraits* (1887)—had been, therefore, not to describe directly some outer reality of time and flux but to create indirectly within his texts the ground of experience. The nonlinear pattern of his prose served both as a metaphor of and an instrument in that pursuit and approach to pure synchronic duration.

In both *The Renaissance* and *Marius,* with their longer sustained arguments, the visionary center invoked by a systematic interplay of one level of the text with another is symbolized by Lady Lisa and Saint Cecilia. Lisa and Cecilia, together with such other mythical figures as Cupid, Isis, and Medusa, are expressive of neither good nor evil, generation nor decay, but of the perpetual dialectic between these differential relations. They are images of a reality which refuses to be wholly unveiled—either looked at directly (Medusa, Cupid, Isis) or possessed through marriage (Cecilia) or definitively interpreted (Lisa). Within the reflexive structure of the text these figures can be felt, glimpsed, even loved. Yet, at first glance, these ideal visions would seem to elude the web of words woven by the imagination to catch them. In the bewildering subjectivities of perception there seems to be an absence of fixed identity, physical and psychic; an impenetrability of lives and objects external to one's self-englobed consciousness; and a radical failure of the past and future to coinhere either in the now of consciousness or in the eternal mind of God. Defining the temporal flux in Heraclitean terms, the Conclusion to *The Renaissance* states boldly (too boldly for the Oxford of 1873) that the impressions of experience "are in perpetual flight; that each of them is limited by time, and that as time is infinitely divisible, each of them is infinitely divisible also; all that is actual in it being a single moment, gone while we try to apprehend it, of which it may ever be more truly said that it has ceased to be than that it is. To such a tremulous wisp constantly re-forming itself on the stream, to a single sharp impression, with a sense in it, a relic more or less fleeting, of such moments gone by, what is real in our life fines itself down" (*Renaissance*, 235–36). Pater's definition of the "relic" bears a striking resemblance to what Jacques Derrida calls the "trace" of an absent reality or ground of origin.[1] Derrida's trace does not mark a reality that was once present and later disappeared; rather, it signifies a reality that was never constituted except reciprocally by an equally phantom trace, an earlier indirect sign or relic. One illusory "origin" thus serves as the source of another in an infinite regression; the ground of thought and experience is never present; only a relic, trace, or reflection of that absent plenitude seems to inhere in the evanescent moments. To use the now-familiar distinction of Ferdinand de Saussure, no signified has ever existed in its own right as the origin of the signifier; meaning is generated only by the interplay of one sound or signifier with another. For such reason, "Words," so Pater quotes Montaigne as saying, "language itself, and therewith the more intimate physiognomy of thought, 'slip every day through our fingers' " (*Gaston*, 102).

This failure of the imperfect, unwieldy web of words to catch more than a trace of a reality external to one's own perceptions obsesses Pater and his hero Marius:

> Our knowledge is limited to what we feel, he reflected: we need no proof that we feel. But can we be sure that things are at all like our feelings? Mere peculiarities in the instruments of our cognition, like the little

1. Derrida, *Of Grammatology*, trans. Gayatri Spivak (Baltimore: Johns Hopkins University Press, 1974), pp. xvii, 61. A propos of Pater's mythic figures, one might observe that Emmanuel Levinas's Thalmudic understanding of the ineffable name of Jehovah within the Tetragrammaton links Heidegger's analysis of being to Derrida's notion of the trace.

knots and waves on the surface of a mirror, may dis-
tort the matter they seem but to represent. Of other
people we cannot truly know even the feelings, nor
how far they would indicate the same modifications,
each one of a personality really unique, in using the
same terms as ourselves; that "common experience,"
which is sometimes proposed as a satisfactory basis of
certainty, being after all only a fixity of language.
[*Marius*, 1: 138]

The imagination may indeed be a mirror which transmutes
life into golden words (1: 180–81), but in terms of any representational description, it is a distorting mirror. Asserted
here, almost a century ago, is the current rejection of the conventional assumption that fiction can re-create reality by a
mere reflection or illusion of external impressions. Heraclitus, says Pater, had also noted that "what the uncorrected
sense gives was a false impression of permanence or fixity in
things, which have really changed their nature in the very
moment in which we see and touch them" (1: 129). And in
the very Heraclitean Conclusion, Pater speaks of analyzing
the world "not of objects in the solidity with which language
invests them, but of impressions, unstable, flickering, inconsistent, which burn and are extinguished with our consciousness of them" (*Renaissance*, 235). Certainly it is not
surprising that Socrates had "doubts as to the power of
words to convey thoughts" (*Plato*, 88) or that Aurelius "with
an extraordinary innate susceptibility to words—*la parole
pour la parole*, as the French say—despairs, in the presence of
Fronto's rhetorical perfection" (*Marius*, 1: 224). Still, Pater has
little but contempt for Fronto and his audience: "amateurs of
exquisite language" (2: 5). Elsewhere he characterizes this
facile rhetoric (the equivalent of representational art) as "a
kind of bastard art of mere words" (*Plato*, 118).

In Pater's own handling of words, the principal singularity apart from its nonlinear syntax is, at least for the fiction, the absence of dialogue. One could, if one wished, refer this feature back to Pater's myth of the Dioscuri in which the brothers exist alternately, not face to face. The solipsistic prison does not allow an unmediated relationship, direct vision akin to Psyche's error of trying to see Cupid. Whenever language attempts to capture reality directly, experience is falsified, reality escapes, and the speaker is betrayed. In *Marius* the single instance of dramatic dialogue (dramatic, in contradistinction to the literary dialogue within translations) itself comments on the failure of language to transcend time and death. " 'Is it a comfort,' " Marius asks the dying Flavian, " 'that I shall often come and weep over you?'—'Not unless I be aware, and hear you weeping!' " (*Marius,* 1: 119). Dialogue remains in the external world as something spoken face to face, never to be caught in Pater's text except indirectly as a "second flowering after date."[2] At the verbal center of the first chapter of *Marius,* the imposition occurs at the rite of the Ambarvalia of "absolute stillness, all persons, even the children, abstaining from speech after the utterance of the pontifical formula, *Favete linguis!*—Silence! Propitious Silence!" (1: 7–8). Enclosing the silence of the worshipers is the unintelligible jumble of consecrated words with the aim of propitiating the gods and renewing fertility; in effect, turning sterility back upon fertility, as portrayed mythically by the sacrifice and return of Polydeuces, by the alternation of the winter and summer Dionysus, or by the loss and return of Persephone to Demeter (these last two deities of vine and corn are carried in the procession). A more elaborate ceremony of the same sort occurs in "Denys l'Auxerrois" with the exhumation of the saint. There the fasting worship-

2. Pater, "Poems by William Morris," p. 300.

ers are engulfed in "a surging sea of lugubrious chants"
(*Imaginary Portraits,* 69). Silence and fasting have cleared the
ground, but neither consecrated jumble nor lugubrious chant
is able to summon the mysterious reality. Instead of a visionary center, there is for Marius only a "solitude . . . almost
painfully complete, as if the nearness of those angry clouds
shut him up in a close place alone in the world" (*Marius,* 1:
12), and for the citizens of Auxerre, absurdly, "a dwindled
body, shrunken inconceivably, but still with every feature of
the face traceable in a sudden oblique ray of ghastly dawn"
(*Imaginary Portraits,* 69).

Yet, if the center remains stubbornly absent despite the
best efforts of priestly language to call it forth, words are still
the only tools with which man can effect his escape from the
solipsistic predicament. If in the rituals of White-nights and
Auxerre there is an absence at the verbal center, then perhaps one ought not to try to force Demeter's daughters or
the brothers Dioscuri to come face to face. In the place of
impotent jumble and chant, Pater would locate a particular
kind of linguistic structure able to create that decentered
ground indirectly. For Pater, the mythic dialectic becomes
inscribed within the reflexive structure of the text itself. Ac-
cepting the fact that literature transposes experience into the
unreality of verbal conception and dramatizing this necessary inadequacy, Pater's art perpetually turns objective reality (the world without) back upon the subjectivities of the
world within and then turns that world back upon the outer,
each pole establishing itself as at once the origin and the
repetition of the other. Although even the text cannot fix
the ultimate ground of the perpetual flux at a permanent
nexus of signification, its reflexive structures can approach
reality asymptotically, constituting within the flux a continuity and duration.

The image of Mona Lisa as she appears in Pater's essay on Leonardo da Vinci (*Renaissance*, 123–26) expresses this reciprocal or reflexively structured relationship in which reality is colored with the imagination and the imagination takes on qualities of the real. In the first paragraph, Pater's description deliberately confounds the origin of her image with its repetition: "As often happens with works in which invention seems to reach its limit, there is an element in it given to, not invented by, the master." Did Verrocchio dream "the unfathomable smile" even before the lady was born? And Lisa herself, second wife of an obscure citizen of Florence, how could she have existed independently of, if not prior to, Leonardo's ideal imaginative dream of feminine beauty: "What was the relationship of a living Florentine to this creature of his thought? By what strange affinities had the dream and the person grown up thus apart, and yet so closely together?" Dream and person, "apart" yet "together": the real and its reflection, the origin and its repetition, exist like the Dioscuri in a reflexive dialectic of "strange affinities." By the repeated "and" at the beginning of successive lines in the climactic sentence of Pater's description, the syntax also makes a point; its exotic epanaphora stresses the connectedness, the perpetual turning back upon each other, of the antinomies of subject and object and their echoing substructure of juxtaposed and contrasting terms: life and death, new and old, innocence and evil, Christian and pagan, pleasure and pain, knowledge and mystery, light and dark, love and lust. As "all," Lisa is neither Helen nor Mary but their mother(s); for like Demeter, she is the maternal source of a sexuality both destructive (Helen or Persephone) and innocent (Mary or Kore). Likewise, later in *Marius the Epicurean*, Pater's protagonist does not so much reject the harlot (Venus and the assorted courtesans of the novel) in order to find the virgin (Psyche) as perceive that in Cecilia corruption and purity coalesce as, mythically, Persephone and Kore coalesce within the greater mother Demeter.

In her reflexive capacity, Mona Lisa also might be instructively compared with the figure of Isis in *Marius*. In the procession of Isis, after the marshals, musicians, and attendants, came "the mirror-bearers of the goddess, carrying large mirrors of beaten brass or silver, turned in such a way as to reflect to the great body of worshippers who followed, the face of the mysterious image, as it moved on its way, and their faces to it, as though they were in fact advancing to meet the heavenly visitor. . . . Then, borne upon a kind of platform, came the goddess herself" (*Marius*, 1: 106–07). Though they may never reach the divine presence (that is, attain the ground of being directly), Isis is yet there, bracketing her worshipers before and behind. By coming to meet the advancing reflection of the goddess who literally follows them (in earlier editions, Pater described the mirrors as reflecting "the face of the sacred image, as it *advanced* on its way"),[3] the worshipers enact the pursuit of an ideal perpetually moving away from their present into the past or the future. This open center of vision, of a before and a behind focused in the silver mirrors, is in sharp contrast to the medieval world and its "absence of the beloved." Describing medieval religion as a "beautiful disease or disorder of the senses," Pater explains that the object of love, the ideal but sensuous form of the divine, "was absent or veiled, not limited to one supreme plastic form like Zeus at Olympia or Athena in the Acropolis, but distracted, as in a fever dream, into a thousand symbols and reflections." With the visible object gone, the emotions were directed instead toward an

3. Pater, *Marius the Epicurean: His Sensations and Ideas,* 2nd ed. (London: Macmillan, 1885), 1: 107; emphasis added.

imaginary object, giving rise to a "passion of which the out-
lets are sealed," so that the senses redound upon the mind
and "the things of nature begin to play a strange delirious
part."[4] Mona Lisa, like Zeus or Athena or Isis—or like the
gemlike flame which is "the focus where the greatest number
of vital forces unite in their purest energy" (*Renaissance*,
236)—represents a converging of the scattered reflections, the
mirror-focus where a thousand reflections are reunited and
begin to "burn."

The fundamental difference between Lady Lisa and the
gods and goddesses of antiquity is that she has a knowledge
of history they do not possess; she embodies a consciousness
which is conscious of itself. In *The Idea of History*, R. G. Collingwood spoke of Pater's "blunder" by including in *The
Renaissance* a chapter on Winckelmann, who "conceived a
profoundly original idea, the idea that there is a history of art
itself, developing through the work of successive artists,
without their conscious awareness of any such development.
The artist, for this conception, is merely the unconscious ve-
hicle of a particular stage in the development of art."[5] But, of
course, it is exactly this "growing revelation of the mind to
itself" (230) that Pater saw as the new turn that European
literature took in the Renaissance. The portrait of Joachim du
Bellay, preceding the essay on Winckelmann, prepared the
way for the inclusion of the latter's historical vision. "If
anywhere the Renaissance became conscious, as a German
philosopher might say, if ever it was understood as a systematic movement by those who took part in it, it is in this
little book [*La deffense et illustration de la langue françoyse*] of
Joachim du Bellay's" (160). As the culmination of a chro-

4. Pater, "Poems by William Morris," p. 302.
5. Collingwood, *The Idea of History* (London: Oxford University Press,
1946), p. 88 n. 1.

nological progression, Winckelmann is present in the Preface and Conclusion of the contemporary Oxford world of "the aesthetic critic" (viii). But within the geographical symmetry of the volume—the Oxford world bracketing the essays on Italian art which themselves are bracketed by essays on the earlier and later French Renaissance— Winckelmann the German is an extraneous interpolation. His marginal stance, however, is precisely the decentered presence that Mona Lisa also shares, incommensurable with the scope of ancient art, overflowing her borders. Indeed, this reflexively self-aware Mona Lisa, Pater's Mona Lisa, is Winckelmann's creation insofar as Winckelmann's work modified Pater's conception of history.

In antique art, limited to concrete sight and touch, to pure form, as Pater described it in his essay on Winckelmann, there is no inner self-awareness to fuse with an outer world. Or rather, in contrast to the "exaggerated inwardness" (205) of Fra Angelico's Virgin Mother, the Venus of Melos "is in no sense a symbol, a suggestion, of anything beyond its own victorious fairness. The mind begins and ends with the finite image, yet loses no part of the spiritual motive. . . . The Greek mind had advanced to a particular stage of self-reflexion, but was careful not to pass beyond it" (205–06). Venus is unquestionably *there*, in the art, as Isis is present in her religious procession: a divine presence shimmering within the warp and woof of time and space. But an antagonism between sense and spirit appeared in the development of culture: "the artist steeps his thought again and again into the fire of colour. To the Greek this immersion in the sensuous was, religiously, at least, indifferent. Greek sensuousness, therefore, does not fever the conscience: it is shameless and childlike. Christian asceticism, on the other hand, discrediting the slightest touch of sense, has from time to time provoked into strong emphasis the contrast or antagonism to itself, of the artistic life, with its inevitable sensuousness" (221–22). Mona Lisa is conscious of that antagonism, and the "sense of shame or loss" lacking in pagan consciousness is present in her. Pater quotes Hegel's description of " 'Phryne, who, as the most beautiful of women, ascended naked out of the water, in the presence of assembled Greece' " and adds that "in the perplexed currents of modern thought . . . the eternal problem of . . . unity with one's self . . . could no longer be solved, as in Phyrne ascending naked out of the water, by perfection of bodily form, or any joyful union with the external world: the shadows had grown too long, the light too solemn, for that" (219–20, 228). It is for this reason that Lisa if set beside "one of those white Greek goddesses or beautiful women of antiquity" (125) would trouble them, for although Lisa, like Phyrne, is a presence that has risen "beside the waters" (124), unlike Phyrne she "has been a diver in deep seas, and keeps their fallen day about her" (125)—the shadows of a romantic sadness, of conflict, contrast, antagonism. "Shameless and childlike" Lisa certainly is not, who like Persephone "has been dead many times, and learned the secrets of the grave" (125).

The difference between Isis in the procession and Mona Lisa in Pater's text is the relatively simple reflexiveness of the former. There is a certain childlike directness in the literal presence of the heavenly image on the shoulders of her bearers. And much the same could be said of the literature of antiquity. Pater's Marius, a burgeoning modern mind, reflects on "that old-fashioned, unconscious ease of the early literature, which could never come again" (*Marius*, 1: 56); and subsequently, Pater, quoting a Homeric description, has Marius nostalgically marvel "how poetic the simple incident seemed, told just thus! . . . And one might think there had been no effort in it: that here was but the almost mechanical transcript of a time, naturally, intrinsically, poetic, a time in which one could hardly have spoken at all without ideal effect, or, the sailors pulled down their boat without making a picture in 'the great style,' against a sky charged with marvels" (1: 100–01). But as Pater observed of the Golden Age in the opening paragraph of "Denys l'Auxerrois": "since we are no longer children, we might well question the advantage of the return to us of a condition of life in which, by the nature of the case, the values of things would, so to speak, lie wholly on their surfaces, unless we could regain also the childish consciousness, or rather unconsciousness, in ourselves, to take all that adroitly and with the appropriate lightness of heart" (*Imaginary Portraits,* 47). Surprisingly, Homer too probably shared Marius's wistful backward looking because, though modern thought represented an emphatic deepening of awareness of the past in the present, even for Homer there were no origins and all was repetition: "might the closer student discover even here, even in Homer, the really mediatorial function of the poet, as between the reader and the actual matter of his experience; the poet waiting, so to speak, in an age which had felt itself trite and commonplace enough, on his opportunity for the touch of 'golden alchemy,' or at least for the pleasantly lighted side of things themselves?" (*Marius,* 1: 101).

If "to come face to face with the people of a past age"— that is, face to face with any absent reality or ground of origin—"is as impossible as to become a little child, or enter again into the womb and be born," what is possible is a mediated, mirrored perception.[6] Though the multireflexive interplay between inner and outer textual levels is more indirect than the sort of perception so literally available to the marchers in the procession of Isis, the ground of reality is also equally *there* in Pater's text. In "The School of Giorgione," Pater had spoken of the highest sort of art, which

6. Pater, "Poems by William Morris," p. 307.

presents us with a kind of profoundly significant and
animated instants, a mere gesture, a look, a smile,
perhaps—some brief and wholly concrete moment—
into which, however, all the motives, all the interests and effects of a long history, have condensed
themselves, and which seem to absorb past and future in an intense consciousness of the present. Such
ideal instants the school of Giorgione selects, with
its admirable tact, from that feverish, tumultuously
coloured world of the old citizens of Venice—exquisite pauses in time, in which, arrested thus, we seem
to be spectators of all the fulness of existence, and
which are like some consummate extract or quintes-
sence of life. [*Renaissance*, 150]

Giorgione's gesture, look, or "smile" turns us back to Lady
Lisa's "unfathomable smile." Pater had noted the special
impression in childhood on Leonardo of "the smiling of
women and the motion of great waters" (104). Lisa's smile,
then, gathers not only the smiling faces of Verrocchio but the
smiles of women in Leonardo's actual experience. Like the
motion of the waters beside which she rises, her smile and
the waves are both curves in transit, images of the flux condensed out of the "feverish, tumultuously coloured world."
And like the form of Isis before and behind, the smiles of
Giorgione and Leonardo are self-sustaining images into
which "all the motives, all the interests and effects of a long
history, have condensed themselves, and which seem to absorb past and future in an intense consciousness of the
present."

Because in Lisa a "long history" has been "condensed,"
she is indeed "all"—"the head upon which all 'the ends of
the world are come,' " summing up in herself "all the
thoughts and experience of the world," "all modes of
thought and life" (124–25)—and she stands outside or above

or beyond any finite set of boundaries. Although in her time seems to pause and be arrested, this involves not a subversion or violation of the flux but a genuine arrogation by the perceiver of its unifying ground. Words, after all, have trapped a reality which nearly always escapes and have done so not by describing a symbol and attributing to it some "objective" solidity of external phenomena but by catching its life in an infinite regress which perpetually turns the person back upon the dream and the dream back upon the person. Lisa is at once both real and imaginary, outer and inner, fact and fiction, and, as the ground of all differential relations, is nothing less than consciousness becoming conscious of itself through the structures of language. Within this reflexive pattern of Lisa's image, even the reader plays a role. Since every impression rests on "the concurrence, renewed from moment to moment, of forces parting sooner or later on their ways" (*Renaissance*, 234), each critic's aesthetic experience reorders her intrinsic significance. Verrocchio's sketches have been absorbed by Leonardo's portrait, which is both a copy and a creation of Lisa; afterward, in the history of echoing and reechoing interpretations, Lisa has indeed been dead and reborn many times, each reading reshaped and reconstructed by the next (Vasari, Lanzi, Hazlitt, Stendhal, Michelet, Gautier, Taine), a tradition passing finally to Pater and from Pater to his readers. Thus, in Pater's creation and copy, Vasari's "jesters and singers"—mediated by Swinburne's "lyres" and Rossetti's "harp"[7]—become at first

7. See Swinburne's words, "The languor in her ears of many lyres," in "Laus Veneris" (line 128) and Rossetti's description of the statue *Sappho* by Marochetti in which, he says, she "sits in abject languor, her feet hanging over the rock, her hands left in her lap, where her harp has sunk; its strings have made music assuredly for the last time. The poetry of the figure is like a pang of life in the stone; the sea is in her ears, and that desolate look in her eyes is upon the sea; and her countenance has fallen." *The Works of Dante Gabriel Rossetti*, ed. William M. Rossetti (London: Ellis, 1911), p. 577.

"mimes and flute players" and, then, the "lyres and flutes" of the climactic sentence, subsiding afterward into the title of Edmund Gosse's "On Viol and Flute," only to be copied and renewed by Yeats as outright poetry in his collection of modern verse and echoed yet again in "the fiddles and the flutes" of T. S. Eliot's "Ash Wednesday."[8]

The composition of *The Renaissance* and of *Marius the Epicurean* followed radically differing paths. From "Winckelmann" to "The School of Giorgione," the writing of *The Renaissance* spanned a decade, seven of its essays having appeared separately in the *Westminster* and *Fortnightly* reviews before being collected in a single volume (its revisions, of course, cover the whole period of Pater's creative activity). Treating the life and works of a diverse assortment of figures, its chapters range across several countries and some five hundred years. *Marius*, on the other hand, written intensively between 1881 and 1884 and published the following year in its entirety, focuses on a single mind within a single country and period. Yet *Marius* displays the same striking contrast of a linear, temporal form within a circular, spatial structure as is found in *The Renaissance*. Hence, Marius leaves a home "which throughout the rest of his life he seemed, amid many distractions of spirit, to be ever seeking to regain" (*Marius*, 1: 22), dying at the last aware of "the scent of the new-mown hay" he had known as a child (1: 20; 2: 216). His beginning foreshadows his end, and his end enfolds his beginning. This symmetrical bracketing of the chronological progression of his life suggests the dissolution

8. Unlike Yeats, who began his anthology, *The Oxford Book of Modern Verse*, by printing Pater's purple passage in *vers libre*, Eliot seems to have separated himself from any intentional indebtedness to Pater. Interestingly, in 1890 Pater himself reviewed (in *Essays*, 107–18) Gosse's "On Viol and Flute."

of origins into repetitions, of a reality which refuses wholly
to yield an attainable ground of being apart from the dialectic
between consciousness and language. Just as Pater's prose,
with its conventional commitment to temporal progression,
pertinaciously assumes a nonlinear pattern in order to embody the perpetual dialectic of differential relations, so
*Marius,* by having exterior and interior mirror or contain
each other like Chinese boxes—by deconstructing the boundaries between the author, his characters, the preexisting
texts within the fictional world of the plot, and the reader—
repeats on a larger scale that syntactical outreach toward the
ground of being.

When Pater's youthful readers (the novel was addressed
to the young men possibly misled by the Conclusion) en-
countered in Marius's truant reading of Apuleius's Golden
Book a mirror of their own activity of reading and respond-
ing to Pater's novel, the text is clearly depicting the process of
its own making and of its being read. And if Pater's readers
found themselves reenacting the experiences of his characters, Pater's characters likewise discover themselves to be
reenacting the experiences of the figures in Apuleius's
preexisting text. The two lads "half-buried in a heap of dry
corn, in an old granary" looked around: "How like a picture!
and it was precisely the scene described in what they were
reading, with just that added poetic touch in the book which
made it delightful and select, and, in the actual place, the ray
of sunlight transforming the rough grain among the cool
brown shadows into heaps of gold. What they were intent on
was, indeed, the book of books, the 'golden' book of that
day, a gift to Flavian" (1: 55). Their "actual place" (which, of
course, exists factually only relative to the text they are reading but is imaginary relative to the world of the author
or reader), by being "precisely the scene" described in
Apuleius's book, has lost something of its reality and become

"like a picture," whereas Apuleius's imaginary world gains a measure of reality in the process. The relation of Pater's characters to the figures about which they read is akin to the relation of the waking world to the daytime dreaming of White-nights—white things being " 'ever an afterthought—the doubles, or seconds, of real things, and themselves but half-real, half-material' " (1: 13). If the imagination is a mirror which transmutes life into golden words, then the "actual" sunlight transforming the grain into "heaps of gold" has its double in the " 'golden' book" of Apuleius, transforming everyday life by a "kind of idealising power" so that "the unadorned remainder of it, the mere drift or *débris* of our days, comes to be as though it were not" (1: 54).

This destabilization of the boundaries between inner and outer frames of the narrative is also a feature of the text of Apuleius within Pater's text. Not only does Apuleius's romance present "story within story—stories with the sudden, unlooked-for changes of dreams" (1: 57), but Apuleius's description of one of his heroines—" 'The golden fibre in the hair, the gold thread-work in the gown marked her as the mistress' "—becomes a metaphor of his own stylistic sense of texture and color: "there was something of that kind in his own work" (1: 57). And when, to return to the primary textual level, Marius witnesses the procession of Isis, being "deeply interested in finding the spectacle much as Apuleius had described it in his famous book" (1: 106), Pater suggests, by having Marius first read and afterward see the procession of Isis, that the reading is the originating perspective from which what is seen is then understood. Priority here belongs to art, not life. Moreover, upon meeting Apuleius years later, Marius perceives him—"who was come to seem almost like one of the personages in his own fiction" (2: 76)—in a way akin to his own sense of the antecedence of the imaginary to the real in which "his life had been so like the reading of a romance to him" (1: 25). The dissolving of sources into repetitions takes another somersault at the point of origin by the reader's awareness that Apuleius's art is descriptive of an actual procession and that Marius's firsthand witnessing of it is in reality only a construction of Pater's imagination. Finally, Pater's Oxford readers, trained in the classics as they were, themselves would be "deeply interested" in comparing the original tale of Apuleius with Pater's rewoven version (as some years back two critics did for our generation in scholarly essays).[9] On this level, Marius's transforming memory serves as a paradigm of the role of the author as he selects and rearranges his materials within the novel as a whole. As Apuleius's "famous story composed itself in the memory of Marius, with an expression changed in some ways from the original and on the whole graver" (1: 92), Pater depicts his own activity as the composer of the novel, giving, through the interplay between his voice and the text he is translating, the priority (in imitation of Sainte-Beuve) to self-portraiture.

Pater's dramatization of the composition and reading of his own text through the presentation of Marius's response to Apuleius's text also has its analogue in *Gaston de Latour*. When Gaston moves from Ronsard, whose poetry has been written, to Montaigne and Bruno who are formulating on a pretextual level their works-to-be-written, the reader is no longer dealing simply with Gaston's imaginary relation to a preexisting text but now also with that of Pater, the authorial presence beyond. Montaigne and Bruno, engaged in the act of composition, are analogues *in* Pater's text for the composition *of* his text, as much the creators of Pater's text as created by it. Further, this interlevel somersaulting has an intralevel

9. Eugene Brzenk, "Pater and Apuleius," *Comparative Literature* 10 (1958): 55–60; Paul Turner, "Pater and Apuleius," *Victorian Studies* 3 (1960): 290–96.

equivalent in Pater's back-and-forth narrative strategy, as, for example, in the unpublished description of Raoul's torture-execution. The actual blows themselves and the moment of death are timelessly suspended outside the present moment of narration, which begins with a description of the crowd's varied responses to the boy's suffering, then disconcertingly jumps back to describe Raoul emerging from prison and being stripped and bound to the wheel, next moves into the hush between the first and second blows, and finally leaves the scene with the passing of a rumor through the crowd that the broken, hanging body is dead. Or, in the opening sacrifice of the Ambarvalia in *Marius*, the lad's pity "for the sacrificial victims and their looks of terror, rising almost to disgust at the central act of the sacrifice itself, a piece of everyday butcher's work," precedes the blessing of the fields "as the procession approached the altars" (1: 9). Or again, in the pivotal slaughter spectacle in "Manly Amusement," one would imagine that the arena, "decked and in order for the first scene" (1: 236), would precede "certain great red patches" (1: 235) of blood on the sand, but, in fact, the descriptions within Pater's narrative are reversed. This achronological quality is not limited to scenes of slaughter; in other ways also, origins dissolve within the verbal texture of the narration into repetitions. For example, the refrain of Flavian's poem, the *Pervigilium veneris*, is a repetition within his verse of a popular song of the streets; also, within the poem it repeats itself as a refrain; and finally, with its twofold repetition of "cras" and its fourfold repetition of the motif of love, its internal elements repeat themselves. Allusions within the text also participate in this achronological quality: Flavian's poetry seems to anticipate the music of the Middle Ages, and Marius emerges from the catacombs "like a later mystic traveller through similar dark places 'quieted by hope,' into the daylight" (2: 104).

This destabilization of categories and levels was announced in *Marius* at its outset by the epigraph. Pater had chosen for his epigraph a quotation from the seventeenth paragraph of Lucian's *The Dream:* "A dream in wintertime, when the nights are longest." To whose dream does the epigraph refer? Marius's? Pater's? the reader's? Or, to approach from another direction, *what* specific dream does Pater ask his readers to entertain? Presumably that of the novel, though one must also remember that *in* the novel at Whitenights Marius does a lot of "dreaming even in the daytime" (1: 14) and that *outside* the plot the reader experiences a dreamlike sensation as he encounters in Marius's discovery of Apuleius's book a mirror of his activity as a reader; that is, his reading activity by being turned back upon itself is swallowed up by the fiction and he feels his own existence as surreal. To call the novel a dream is to affirm its nature as artifice, to label it an imaginary creation, to see it not as a construct which aspires to substitute for reality or masquerade in the place of outer experience (as conventional illusionistic fiction does) but as a structure perpetually turning back upon itself, as something which is at once both real and imaginary, outer and inner, fact and fiction. The fixed antagonism that conventional fiction accepts as permanent between the real and the imaginary and that it attempts to bridge by a willing suspension of disbelief, Pater's fiction disavows. Pater places in its stead the model of the dream and its self-reflexive structure, thus creating a work not to contain the quotidian self but to establish an aesthetic or textual self that, as outer experience turns back upon itself in an eternal dialectic in which dreams (fiction) come true, discloses itself as ontologically ab-original (before the originating or quotidian self). The veridical reality of autobiographical experience has been absorbed into or swallowed up by the fiction, a dream, which then establishes itself as an outer reality only to turn back upon itself once again in a perpetual dialectic—each level of dream or reality subsumed in the next frame in or out.

In the essay from which Pater took his epigraph, Lucian's hearers impatiently exclaim: "a winter dream. . . . What got into him to tell us this idle tale and to speak of a night of his childhood and dreams that are ancient and superannuated? . . . Surely he doesn't take us for interpreters of dreams?" But Lucian replies that he told his dream so that his hearers may take the better direction and cleave to education. It is not difficult to see in Pater's choice of epigraph an allusion to the fact that the veiled autobiography of *Marius* was meant to be a corrective to those who misinterpreted the Conclusion to *The Renaissance*. But ironically, by calling his novel a dream, Pater also undercut the possibility for the sort of recantation certain readers expected, for the reflexive dream structure offers a vision of the flux equal to that of *The Renaissance*. His recognition that the categories of space and time, identity and memory, are insubstantial and relative dictated for him a unique kind of fiction which swallowed up veridical reality. Verisimilitude, says Pater, lies not in the story of a struggle with some limiting force external to the psyche but with the psyche's intrinsic limitation and sense of ontological vertigo: the "shaken tapestry" (*Gaston*, 124). As it is structured, the text prohibits the ontological grounding of any single level at the expense of another; instead, it becomes a mirror constantly transforming (or metamorphosing, to borrow the term from Apuleius's prominently featured romance and to point out another self-referential gesture of the novel) inner and outer in a ceaseless shuttling back and forth between all possible levels—a regression and progression ad infinitum. The text is a work whose drama lies always in the interchange between inner and outer frames and whose ground situation, like the mirrored image of Isis before and after, is always deferred to some frame yet further in or further out. The reader feels lost within a vertiginously arch structure of interweaving levels of illusion and fact. Which is the ground situation? the plot? the author's life? or the reader's experience of the text?

Yet neither Pater nor his heroes are emotionally impotent, doomed to some sterile isolation, for though the progressions and regressions within the text may defer final meaning, they do not abolish it completely. Pater does not deny a falling short in the self's outreach toward an ungraspable reality; but in the mutual enhancement of one dialectical term by the other, he denies universal final defeat. He remarks of culture generally that "the reserve of the elder generation exquisitely refined by the antagonism of the new" is an important aspect in the development of "the human spirit on its way to perfection" (*Appreciations*, 65). And on the personal level, by the surrender of the authorial life to the imaginary Other, the text exerts an idealizing influence on its quotidian genitor: " 'the soul takes colour from its fantasies' " (*Marius*, 2: 38), Pater quotes Aurelius as saying. So also Leonardo's originals have been modified by the copyist, "and these variations have but brought out the more the purpose, or expression of the original" (*Renaissance*, 118). Or again: "The beauty of the *palaestra*, and the beauty of the artist's workshop, reacted on one another. The youth tried to rival his gods; and his increased beauty passed back into them" (209). Also, the recomposition of Apuleius's tale in Marius's memory, changed "and on the whole graver" (ugliness and brutality are omitted, diction and image are refined, cadences are made more musical), is not just a reflexive image of Pater as author but also suggests the idealization of the original in the cultural process. Thus, "to Gaston for one, the power of the old classic poetry itself was explained by the reflex action of the new, and might seem to justify its pretensions at last"

(*Gaston*, 58). Later, admiring his reflection in Jasmin's Venetian mirror, Gaston muses that the image might react on the original, refining it one degree further. The mirror image is especially suggestive here, because when transposed to a textual sphere of meaning it again implies that the image in the mirror, the textual double, justifies or refines one degree further its authorial genitor. Pater defines religion in this fashion as "a sacred history," "a sacred ideal," or "a mirror" which idealizes ordinary life and turns mortals into "angels," into "those sacred personalities, which are at once the reflex and the pattern of our nobler phases of life" (*Miscellaneous Studies*, 193, 194). If one equates literature with scripture, the text (derived from classical Latin via the medieval *textus,* a scriptural text) once again is seen to be an idealizing mirror.

The power of the textual mirror to idealize reality may especially be seen in the symbolism associated with Marius's fear of snakes and with the head of Medusa for which the villa of White-nights was famous. The Medusa of Marius's childhood, like the Medusa of young Leonardo's experience in Pater's retelling of Vasari's anecdote, becomes in Pater's portraiture an allegory of the relation of the author to his text. Central to Pater's intention is the story of how Perseus slew the gorgon by looking at her reflection in his shield and so avoided the petrification of direct gaze. To gaze at the Medusa directly—as Psyche, for example, tried to gaze directly on the forbidden form of Cupid—is simply a loss of vision, a subversion or falsification of the actual character of the flux. Whenever the autobiographer attempts to capture directly that identity signified by the discourse of his text—that unified self seemingly present continuously through time—he distorts experience by claiming for it a specious presence. "Being" cannot be arrested and apprehended "as it is," for this yields only the nihilistic horror

of the petrifying corpse. But Perseus, like the author with the
mirror of his text, catches the reflection in his shield, reproducing the image of mortality in a purified form—and so
renders it harmless. Thus, Leonardo's projections of Medusa
are in artistic form, for Leonardo as Perseus reflects reality's
frightening guises in an aesthetic structure, in an ideal visionary creation in which beauty and horror, life and death,
ceaselessly pass into each other, like the mythic doubles of
Demeter and the Dioscuri. In effect, the perishing self now
has access to an all-encompassing reciprocal interplay which
will never fix its ground of being permanently but, in the
words of the Conclusion, does allow the individual to "pass
most swiftly from point to point, and be present always at
the focus where the greatest number of vital forces unite in
their purest energy. . . . To burn always with this hard, gemlike flame, to maintain this ecstasy, is success in life" (*Renaissance*, 236). In this fashion the love child Leonardo earned his
father's approval: the horror inspired by the real gorgon's
head (his bastardy) has been transformed into the "pretended astonishment" (105–06) of the doting father at his artistic skill.

*Marius* is a novel about the hero's development from a
state of pretextual dreaming to the diaphanous condition of
artistic existence. Initially, Marius's dreams at White-nights
have not as yet found their dialectical counterpart in the
world without. His home of White-nights, says Pater, suggests "nights not of quite blank forgetfulness, but passed in
continuous dreaming, only half veiled by sleep" (*Marius*, 1:
14). Echoing as it does (earlier editions read: "nights *not*
passed *in* quite *blank forgetfulness*," emphasis added) the
"Not in entire forgetfulness" of Wordsworth's "Intimations
Ode," which defines birth as "but a sleep and a forgetting,"
Pater's description of dreamy White-nights suggests a complementary mode to waking existence with an especial po-

tential for ideality. The goddess of this veiled, twilight kingdom is Persephone, who holds "the poppy, emblem of sleep
and death by its narcotic juices, of life and ressurection by its
innumerable seeds, of the dreams, therefore, that may inter-
vene between falling asleep and waking" (*Greek Studies*,
148–49). Whether it be Wordsworth's "clouds of glory" or
Persephone's seeds of "life and resurrection," the dream
within has not as yet found its renewing aesthetic counterpart. One thinks here of Coleridge, the homesick "narcotist,"
as a Marius who failed to achieve the necessary dialectical
synthesis with art, and so as an adult he could never return
to the childhood harmony of home.

The effort to renew with word and phrase had been present at the outset of the novel in the ritual of the purification
of the land at White-nights through the consecrated but unintelligible words of the old liturgy. But in contrast to the
emerging significance of the Mass, its counterpart for Marius
in the latter half of the novel, the unintelligibility of the ritual
grows as it recedes into the past; thus, the impurity of mortality must await its first major verbal chastening when the
sick Marius is healed at the temple of Aesculapius. Just as the
mortal condition is idealized by its textual double (Medusa/
mortality is rendered harmless by Perseus/author), so
Marius's snake-dream at the temple is refracted and purified
by the priestly utterance. The speaker's

> expression of perfect temperance had in it a fascinat-
> ing power—the merely negative element of purity, the
> mere freedom from taint or flaw, in exercise as a pos-
> itive influence. . . . It was as a weighty sanction of
> such temperance, in almost visible symbolism (an
> outward imagery identifying itself with unseen mo-
> ralities) that the memory of that night's double ex-
> perience, the dream of the great sallow snake and the

utterance of the young priest, always returned to him,
and the contrast therein involved made him revolt
with unfaltering instinct from the bare thought of an
excess in sleep, or diet, or even in matters of taste, still
more from any excess of a coarser kind. [*Marius*, 1:
33–34]

These contrasting doubles of snaky dream and priestly discourse are imagistically restated in the holy well of the temple: "From the rim of its basin rose a circle of trim columns to
support a cupola of singular lightness and grace, itself full of
reflected light from the rippling surface, through which
might be traced the wavy figure-work of the marble lining
below as the stream of water rushed in. Legend told of a visit
of Aesculapius to this place, earlier and happier than his first
coming to Rome: an inscription around the cupola recorded
it in letters of gold. 'Being come unto this place the son of
God loved it exceedingly' " (1: 35). Like the presence of Isis
in Apuleius's procession, the light of Apollo's son is reflected
by the mirror of the pure water; and the snakes associated
with him are transfigured in the serpentine pattern beneath
the rippling surface. Waves of water superimposed upon
waves of figure-work are like the snakes of Medusa, as described by Pater in Leonardo's picture, which break in waves
upon her stone brow, a brow like the marble rim of Aesculapius's well. The inscribed cupola, purified of the
Medusean snakes of mortality and full of reflected light from
the mirroring water, resembles the reflexive text in which the
author's marginal existence seeks its point of equilibrium.

These subtle relationships are dramatized for Marius in a
culminating visionary experience at Aesculapius's shrine:
"just before his departure the priest . . . lifting a cunningly
contrived panel, which formed the back of one of the carved
seats, bade him look through. What he saw was like the vi-

sion of a new world, by the opening of some unsuspected window in a familiar dwelling-place" (1: 40). Earlier, in "The Child in the House," Pater had suggested that certain exquisite moments of more-than-temporal dimension can release the imprisoned dream from the immuring subjectivities of the mind. The open gate through which the child passes to obtain the vision of the hawthorn—foreshadowed in the release of the starlings and restated in Florian's rescue of his pet bird from the closed house (Leonardo too frees caged birds, linking him imagistically to this autobiographical portrait)—symbolizes Florian's escape from that solipsistic predicament described in those familiar words from the Conclusion to *The Renaissance:* "Experience, already reduced to a group of impressions, is ringed round for each one of us by that thick wall of personality through which no real voice has ever pierced on its way to us, or from us to that which we can only conjecture to be without. Every one of those impressions is the impression of the individual in his isolation, each mind keeping as a solitary prisoner its own dream of a world" (*Renaissance,* 235). Marius's experience at the Sabine inn, although passing beyond the bounds of his immediate visible experience, is clearly meant to develop the visionary possibilities for escape suggested at the Aesculapian shrine (with the word *reflections* not excluding overtones of a textual mirroring): "Might not this entire material world, the very scene around him, the immemorial rocks, the firm marble, the olive-gardens, the falling water, be themselves but reflections in, or a creation of, that one indefectible mind, wherein he too became conscious, for an hour, a day, for so many years? . . . The purely material world, that close, impassable prison-wall [earlier: "heavy wall," clearly an analogue to the "thick wall of personality" in the Conclusion], seemed just then the unreal thing, to be actually dissolving away all around him" (*Marius,* 2: 69–70). On the one hand, the "indefectible mind" is an expression of collective humanity; on the other, it is the text in its all-encompassing reflexive nature.

Although escape from an imprisoning subjectivity lies largely within the domain of art, not all artistic expression is capable of reaching what Pater in the Conclusion described as the goal "to set the spirit free for a moment" (*Renaissance*, 237). A representational art that copies an exterior reality rather than mirrors an inner vision is an art of entrapping walls, an art of only illusory openings. Prior to his first audience with the emperor, Marius admires the decoration on the walls: "In the midst of one of them was depicted, under a trellis of fruit you might have gathered, the figure of a woman knocking at a door with wonderful reality of perspective" (*Marius*, 1: 213). Not coincidentally, in this room with the illusory door the assassins of Caligula sought "refuge after the murder" (2: 33); like all merely representational art, the walls are simply a deceitful trompe l'oeil and call up associations of that madness inherent in the closed environment without outlet or escape. And when Marius finally enters Aurelius's presence, he discovers a chamber to match the illusory door, a room nearly "windowless" with only a "quite medieval window here and there" (1: 216) to let in light. In a crossed-out passage in the fragmentary essay, "Art and Religion," Pater spoke of "the great central prayer of this generation, to put ourselves in the way of light we so greatly desire—in the 'way of hope'—the point where things may look less confused than they do." Only some such visionary work, like the lifting of "a cunningly contrived panel" as at the shrine of Aesculapius or the image of Cecilia herself, can approach, if not completely attain to, that "open passage" leading from the "sleepy" dreamworld of the solitary cell "to things as they are in themselves, to absolute realities."[10]

10. Pater, "Art and Religion," Houghton Library, Harvard University: bMS Eng 1150 (11); "Moral Philosophy," bMS Eng 1150 (17).

In the diptych, "Two Curious Houses," Cecilia's villa is
contrasted with the villa at Tusculum. At Tusculum, reality
had remained for Marius opaque; there had been in Cicero's
villa no analogue to that "opening of an unsuspected window in some familiar dwelling-place" as had occurred at the
shrine of Aesculapius: "the numerous cascades of the pre-
cipitous garden of the villa, framed in the doorway of the
hall, fell into a harmless picture, in its place among the pictures within, and scarcely more real than they" (2: 77). At
first sight there is little in the scene at either the Temple of
Aesculapius or the villa at Tusculum that would distinguish
one vista from the other, making the one a vision of a new
world, the other harmless and unreal. But what is missing
from the latter is an authentic visionary center, not to be
supplied by Apuleius's fantastic musings: " 'Has nature
connected itself together by no bond, allowed itself to be
thus crippled, and split into the divine and human elements?' he inquires and replies: 'Well! there are certain
divine powers of a middle nature, through whom our aspirations are conveyed to the gods, and theirs to us.' " But
Marius cannot accept such quasi-Platonic angels: "For himself, it was clear, he must still hold by what his eyes really
saw" (2: 88–90). In Saint Cecilia and the church in her house,
Marius finds a relational interplay surpassing Apuleius's
fantasies, arranged, "as if in designed congruity with his
favourite precepts of the power of physical vision, into an
actual picture" (2: 97). Here the full significance of Marius's
visions at the Temple of Aesculapius and at the Sabine inn is
made explicit; for Cecilia, like Lady Lisa in *The Renaissance*,
is the visionary center between dialectical opposites. She is
both in the novel and a symbol of it and thus offers an escape
from the particularities of time and place.

At a "cross-road" Marius enters "a doorway in a long,
low wall" (2: 94) to find himself in the garden of Saint
Cecilia's house. Life turns back upon art as the old flower

garden with its venerable olive trees (echoing the olives in
the garden at the Sabine inn and the aged hawthorn in the
garden of "The Child in the House") formed "a picture in
pensive shade and fiery blossom, as transparent, under that
afternoon light, as the old miniature-painters' work on the
walls of the chambers within" (2: 98). Central to this scene is
Cecilia, herself compared to a statue (2: 105), whom Marius
sees after his descent into the catacombs within the precincts
of her garden. Marius's own sense "of regeneration, of escape from the grave" (2: 103), begins with his Dantesque
reascent from their underworld; and with her appearance his
"visionary scene" is fully composed:

> A few minutes later, passing forward on his way along
> the public road, he could have fancied it a dream. . . .
> In truth, one of his most characteristic and constant
> traits had ever been a certain longing for escape—for
> some sudden, relieving interchange, across the very
> spaces of life, it might be, along which he had lingered
> most pleasantly—for a lifting, from time to time, of
> the actual horizon. It was like the necessity under
> which the painter finds himself, to set a window or
> open doorway in the background of his picture. . . .
> Rome and Roman life, just then, were come to seem
> like some stifling forest of bronze-work, transformed,
> as if by malign enchantment, out of the generations of
> living trees, yet with roots in a deep, down-trodden
> soil of poignant human susceptibilities. In the midst
> of its suffocation, that old longing for escape had been
> satisfied by this vision of the church in Cecilia's
> house, as never before. [2: 105–06]

The Dantean forest or malign Circean enchantment can be
escaped only by Cecilia's reflexive dialectic. The twice-
repeated "escape" and such phrases as "relieving inter-

change," "lifting . . . of the . . . horizon," and "open doorway" are all by now familiar as images of a visionary or
reflexive art. Especially the sudden "interchange"—the
mutual changing of "spaces" between new and old—
evokes Cecilia's role as a double goddess. When Marius later encounters her burying a child in the underworld
of the catacombs, she, no less than Lady Lisa, explicitly embodies the ceaselessly interacting antinomies of generation and decay.

Prefacing this vision of Cecilia and the church in her
house, Pater quotes a "mystical German writer" on the relation of the soul to the house in which it dwells—a passage
cited earlier in chapter 1, which continues: "and the light
which creeps at a particular hour on a particular picture or
space upon the wall, the scent of flowers in the air at a particular window, become to her, not so much apprehended
objects, as themselves powers of apprehension and doorways to things beyond—the germ or rudiment of certain new
faculties, by which she, dimly yet surely, apprehends a matter lying beyond her actually attained capacities of spirit and
sense" (2: 93). By virtue of the interchange between dialectical poles, objects become "doorways to things beyond" both
"spirit and sense." Such openings are generated by the kind
of "intelligible relationships" that Pater had found described
in the thought of Heraclitus: "In this 'perpetual flux' of
things and of souls, there was, as Heraclitus conceived, a
continuance, if not of their material or spiritual elements, yet
of orderly intelligible relationships, like the harmony of
musical notes, wrought out in and through the series of their
mutations—ordinances of the divine reason, maintained
throughout the changes of the phenomenal world; and this
harmony in their mutation and opposition, was, after all, a
principle of sanity, of reality, there" (1: 131). Any ground of
reality will lie not in elements material or spiritual but in

the relationships objectively established between them—
ultimately for Pater by the text.

The visionary center able to open the rigid, closed struc-
tures of the lifeless form became a central theme in the volume of *Imaginary Portraits* (1887) published shortly after
*Marius.* A collection whose format was possibly inspired by
Flaubert's *Trois contes* and the style of whose portraits owed a
debt to the critical method of Sainte-Beuve's *Portrait littéraire,*
Pater's volume contained "A Prince of Court Painters,"
"Denys l'Auxerrois," "Sebastian van Storck," and "Duke
Carl of Rosenmold." To achieve maximum contrast of theme,
mood, and chronology among the four works, Pater both altered the original order of their publication and rejected a
chronological arrangement. In a sense, the substructure of
juxtapositions and contrasts in *Marius* here becomes the
dominant ordering principle; and although the volume
clearly cannot offer a single, all-embracing visionary center,
each of the portraits explores an aspect of the contrasting artistic modes of representation or vision, and the figures in
each portrait can be rated by their success or failure in at-
taining to the open passage of visionary art. But even though
deprived of an all-embracing symbol for the visionary focus,
*Imaginary Portraits* still contains the central presence of the
author himself beyond the overt symbol. The volume does
not so much describe a middle-aged don with artistic sen-
sibilities and a love of cats as inscribe in virtually every position within its portraits a psychic and hidden Pater who
awaits his reader as the middle term among all their differing
layers of meaning. When Pater quotes Lamb to the effect that
" 'I cannot make these present times . . . present to *me*,' " he
implies the unreality of the present except as it interacts with
the past. Unable to participate directly in present life, Pater
affirms the reciprocal dependence of past and present within

the creative act: his present self finds its standing ground in the rounding out of a fragmentary record from the past. Each tale originates in an imaginary text or quasi-text (a journal, a storytelling tapestry, old letters and bones like confused lines of script) seemingly discovered in the course of the author's scholarly pursuits. Out of these fragments of fact and fiction, Pater then proceeds to reconstruct portraits that reflect his intellectual preoccupations and personal tensions.

"I have a fancy always," says the narrator of Pater's first published portrait, "A Prince of Court Painters," "that I may meet Antony Watteau there again, any time; just as, when a child, having found one day a tiny box in the shape of a silver coin, for long afterwards I used to try every piece of money that came into my hands, expecting it to open" (*Imaginary Portraits*, 25). Unlike her magical coin, the church of Saint Vaast, which promised to disclose the object of her love, Antony Watteau, unfortunately turns out to be a trap for the bird-soul: "a small bird . . . had flown into the church but could find no way out again. I suspect it will remain there, fluttering round and round distractedly, far up under the arched roof, till it dies exhausted. . . . —human life may be like that bird too!" (14–15). Her sense of spatial entrapment is matched by a sense of temporal entrapment also: "how to get through time becomes sometimes the question,—unavoidably; though it strikes me as a thing unspeakably sad in a life so short as ours" (25). Since Marie-Marguerite cannot possess Watteau, she takes her brother's art, because of its nearness to that of Watteau, "as the central interest of my life. I bury myself in that" (26). But her "bury" is ominous, suggestive not of openings, but of final closures, of, for example, those tombs along the Appian Way in *Marius*. Unlike Watteau, whose painted "walls seem to cry out:—No! to make delicate insinuation, for a music, a conversation, nimbler than any we have known, or are likely to

find here" (21), the ambition of Jean-Baptiste, Marie-Marguerite's brother, is to render competently "a solid and
veritable likeness" (27) of everyday life. This leaves brother
and, perforce, sister immured within "that close, impassable
prison-wall" of representational fixity—Jean-Baptiste unaware, Marie-Marguerite suffocating. "As for me," exclaims
Marie-Marguerite, "I suffocate this summer afternoon in this
pretty *Watteau* chamber of ours, where Jean-Baptiste is at
work so contentedly" (104).

One wonders how much of himself and his sisters Pater
saw in this relationship of M. and Mlle Pater (from whose
family he claimed descent). In the rejected Jean-Baptiste,
who reestablished a filial relationship with the remote Watteau only upon the latter's death, we have a reflection of Pater's own craving for an absent paternal figure. And in her
"immobility of disposition" (28) as well as in her frustrated
admiration for a charismatic artistic figure, Marie-Marguerite, the writer, may reflect Pater. By projecting himself into both brother and sister, Pater can suggest simultaneously his frustration at being a mere belated imitator of
original genius, like Jean-Baptiste, and also his impatience at
being condemned to living without companionship of a high
artistic order, like Marie-Marguerite. Pater's personal presence here is reinforced by a reflexivity similar to that of
Apuleius's text within *Marius*. In the journal entry of October
1717, the heroine is reading the Abbé Prévost's novel, *Manon
Lescaut*, and observes that "this is the book those fine ladies
in Watteau's 'conversations,' who look so exquisitely pure,
lay down on the cushion when the children run up" (37). But
in putting the book the heroine reads into a picture the
heroine sees, the text hints at the fictitious aspect of her own
existence by associating her level of reality with that of the
ladies in the picture. This novel-within-a-portrait, turning
back upon itself as the book the heroine herself reads, also

turns back upon Pater's readers, for it is a book we, too, have reflected upon. Thus characters, author, readers all find their personal identities to be interchangeable in this textual hall of mirrors.

The subtlest symbol of Pater's personal presence in the portrait is the unfinished picture of Marie-Marguerite begun by her beloved Watteau. Never having told her passion, she keeps that purity those "fine ladies" in Watteau's other pictures yielded up. Manon Lescaut, her dark double, implies the absence in her life of an interplay productive of the sort of wholeness that enabled Watteau and Mlle Rosalba to complete portraits of each other. But whereas Watteau is unable to finish Marie-Marguerite's picture, Pater does finish his imaginary "portrait" and thus steps into the plot, so to speak, to become for her the hidden lover, the decentered artist of her desire. This ultimate textual fulfillment is deferred in Watteau's life also. Watteau's walls, unlike those of Jean-Baptiste, cry out for a visionary escape; but he, too, awaits the opening door of communication. His "escape . . . from that blank stone house" (7), like the flight of the bird from the church, has been largely thwarted; he escapes only the physically thick walls of Valenciennes. Though the works he paints may approximate "that impossible or forbidden world which the mason's boy saw through the closed gateways of the enchanted garden" (34)—gardens both in "The Child in the House" and at Cecilia's house that composed for Marius into "an actual picture" are here recalled—"his dream of a better world than the real one" (34–35) remains unsatisfied. Watteau dies, "always a seeker after something in the world that is there in no satisfying measure, or not at all" (44).

For Sebastian van Storck, all of Holland is like the Watteau chamber to Marie-Marguerite: "The heavy summer . . . which, while it gleamed very pleasantly russet and yellow for

the painter Albert Cuyp, seemed wellnigh to suffocate
Sebastian van Storck" (81–82). Sebastian's seeking out "those
prospects *à vol a'oiseau*" (89) is, clearly, a less creative solu-
tion than Watteau's desperate but vain effort to open up the
entrapping walls with his decorations. It suggests instead
Marcus Aurelius's empty palace. Aurelius, to raise funds for
his war, sold the imperial furniture and lived alone in his
hollow rooms: "in his empty house, the man of mind, who
had always made so much of the pleasures of philosophic
contemplation, felt freer in thought than ever" (*Marius*, 2:
36). Sebastian, too, retreats into "a kind of *empty* place"
where "all had been mentally put to rights by the working-
out of a long equation, which had zero is equal to zero for its
result" (*Imaginary Portraits,* 90). Though Sebastian refused to
travel, he did enjoy the "wide wings of space itself" and
covered the four walls of his room with scenes by Philips de
Koninck, "visionary escapes, north, south, east, and west,
into a wide-open though, it must be confessed, a somewhat
sullen land" (89). So great was Sebastian's aversion to entanglement in the warm material life of Holland that he
would not be painted and, when he wrote to anyone, he "left
his very letters unsigned" (100). For Sebastian, wisdom con-
sisted in hastening the "restoration of equilibrium, the calm
surface of the absolute, untroubled mind, to *tabula rasa,* by
the extinction in one's self of all that is but correlative to the
finite illusion—by the suppression of ourselves" (106–07).
One might say that, having discovered the limitations of representational art, Sebastian rejects outright all artistic forms.
Spurning the aesthetic life of Holland, he seeks instead some
tabula rasa suggestive of the blank canvas prior to any art,
either representational or visionary—and a canvas that will
remain, like the letters, unsigned. But for Sebastian, as for
Aurelius, this freedom is illusory; they remain prisoners
locked in their dreams of a world. Aurelius's empty cham-

bers are blankly windowless and Sebastian's ideal place is a frozen waste with "the meadows now lying dead below the ice" (81).

"To restore *tabula rasa* . . . by a continual effort at self-effacement" (110) is a sort of unwitting parody of Pater's own artistic aim. Schiller, in the twenty-second of his *Ästhetische Briefe,* had said that in the pure work—as in music—matter is dissolved in form; and as early as 1864 in "Diaphanéité," Pater attempted to apply this insight to the personality of the aesthetic hero: "The artist and he who has treated life in the spirit of art desires only to be shown to the world as he really is; as he comes nearer and nearer to perfection, the veil of an outer life not simply expressive of the inward becomes thinner and thinner" (*Miscellaneous Studies,* 249). The meaning of the hero's "clear crystal nature" (253) lies in his pure textuality. Later, when writing of Dante, Pater twice uses the image of the crystal in identical sentences to describe this purity of being. In the "vehement and impassioned heat" of Dante's vision, he says, "the material and spiritual are fused and blent; if the spiritual attains the definite visibility of a crystal, what is material loses its earthiness and impurity" (*Appreciations,* 212; *Plato,* 135). Elsewhere, Pater also depicts the transmutation of life into language and art, often mentioning text and life in the same phrase as if they were identical: "the engaging personality in life or in a book" (*Renaissance,* ix); "a vision, almost 'beatific,' of ideal personalities in life and art" (*Marius,* 2: 22). Montaigne's essays, says Pater, "were themselves a life, the power which makes them what they are having been accumulated in them imperceptibly by a thousand repeated modifications, like character in a person" (*Gaston,* 83–84). Although Pater's rhetoric at times may seem to describe Sebastian's "self-effacement" as an ideal, what in fact Pater is talking about is the reconstitution of oneself within the textual Other. When opposites are balanced within the reflexive textual structure, the result is not Sebastian's "zero is equal to zero" but rather a set of differential relationships between a host of inner and outer levels.

In the portraits of Denys l'Auxerrois and Duke Carl of Rosenmold, Pater dramatizes this movement toward the differential mode of textual existence. Just as Pater dissolves his own life and thought in the preexisting text, Carl and Denys channel their lives into differential patterns, becoming trapped thereby as victims of their mythic roles (though ultimately their suffering is, as for Polydeuces, a willed sacrifice). Following an implicit cyclic pattern which grafts pagan myth onto Christian miracle, Denys appears at Easter, making not only the cathedral ball-play "really a game" but also making "life like a stage-play" (*Imaginary Portraits*, 58, 61). This figurative turning of life into art is given literal form in the sequel to the drama of the return of Dionysus in which Denys acts. In the pageant of the "Hunting of Winter," the pretended pursuit becomes actual, and Denys the actor becomes Dionysus the victim. The progressive assimilation of actual life to mythic pattern—as, analogously, in pure art the separation of matter and form is eradicated and replaced by relation—heralds the early French renaissance. This renewal is symbolized by Denys's construction of the organ (music being, as Pater following Schiller had said, that condition toward which all the arts aspire when matter and form coalesce) and is explicitly present in his rejuvenation of an ancient classic text: "It was as if the gay old pagan world had been *blessed* in some way, . . . seen most clearly in the rich miniature work . . . —a marvellous Ovid especially, upon the pages of which those old loves and sorrows seemed to come to life again" (71).

This textual rejuvenation had been prefigured by the immensely old vine that "clothed itself with fruit once more" (62), recalling the aged hawthorn in "The Child in the

House" and the *"aubépine* of immemorial age" in *Gaston*,[11] both of which miraculously flowered as if with a second youth. One might seize upon the single word "immemorial" common to vine and aubepine and, turning back to the "immemorial rocks" among which at the Sabine inn Marius had his vision (mindful also of the rocks among which the even older Mona Lisa sits), connect immemorial age and rocklike hardness with Pater's description in "Romanticism" of "the old, immemorial, well-recognised" (*Appreciations*, 257) classical types. The rejuvenating power of the fluid romantic spirit, "breaking through" (251) the age and hardness of the classic type embodies just that combination of qualities suggested by Pater's image of the hard, gemlike flame and found in Denys's "flask of lively green glass, like a great emerald" (*Imaginary Portraits*, 56) among the ashes of the dead. For Denys is the quintessential figure of romanticism; and his "fondness for oddly grown or even misshapen, yet potentially happy, children" (62), for example, is expressive of what Pater earlier had defined as the romantic sense of pity, delight in "singularity," and a love of "animals and children";[12] and this combines with such a power of rejuvenation that in his presence even the aged Dean felt "suddenly relieved of his burden of eighty years" (58).

In "Romanticism" Pater concedes the element of the grotesque, bizarre, and macabre as being inherent in the extremes of the romantic temperament; but by stressing the harmonious blending in the highest art of classic and romantic motifs, only half of Denys's story is foreshadowed. This is the half portraying the marriage of Ariane to the young count of Chastellux. Ariane's affections had originally been directed toward Denys himself; she wished to "make

11. Pater, *Gaston de Latour*, Houghton Library, Harvard University: bMS Eng 1150 (4), chap. 13.
12. Pater, "Romanticism," *Macmillan's Magazine* 35 (1876): 68.

him son-in-law to the old count her father, old and not long
for this world" (66). Because Ariane's father was also Denys's
father, he being the love child of former days, Ariane is Denys's feminine half; and her marriage to Chastellux is also
Denys's. But if the harmonious reconciliation between the
feuding houses of Chastellux and Auxerre is formalized by
marriage, the renewal of age by youth cannot be achieved
without slaughter. In a sentence suppressed when "Romanticism" was reprinted as the Postscript to *Appreciations*, Pater
had spoken metaphorically of the "flowers" of romanticism
"ripened not by quiet, everyday sunshine, but by the lightning, which, tearing open the hill-side, brought the seeds
hidden there to a sudden, mysterious blossoming."[13] This
"tearing open" is present both at Denys's birth (a Semele-
type genesis with his mother killed by lightning) and again
at his death. The blood on Denys's scratched lip turns the
pretended hunting to a real slaying; in this way, "untranslatable" "ultimate differences" between the dialectical poles are
reconciled, and opposites become able "reciprocally to lend
each other new forces." By his life's blood, Denys becomes
the generative figure in the rebirth of higher culture—the
Renaissance to be. In contrast to the pious but sterile exhumation of the saint's shrunken, ghastly body, the opening of
the coffin at the beginning of Denys's story foretells his rejuvenating death and its yield of stained glass and tapestry
that the cultivated narrator finds on his visit to Auxerre—
those fragments out of which Pater weaves Denys's story
anew and which in turn will be rewoven by yet other artists
or literary critics.

The hero of Pater's "Duke Carl of Rosenmold," an earlier
version of the mad, architecturally and operatically inspired
King Ludwig II of Bavaria, doomed by his court counselors,

13. Ibid., p. 66. As will become apparent in chapter 5 of this study, the
passage was suppressed because of its Baudelairean overtones.

is like Denys a figure of romantic vitality: "he invigorated what he borrowed" (124). Also like Marius, who anticipates in his dying hour some impending revelation, Carl believes that "the literature which might set heart and mind free must exist somewhere, though court librarians could not say where" (130). His preference in music is for those passages of "unending melody—which certainly never came to what could rightly be called an ending here on earth" (132), and he himself longs to be propelled "out of space beyond the Alps or the Rhine, into future time" (143). The absent literature, the unending melody (reminiscent of Watteau's inability to bring his portrait of Marie-Marguerite to a fitting close), the aspiration for future time—all suggest the quest for an un-graspable reality: "A free, open space had been determined, which something now to be created, created by him, must occupy" (145). He seizes upon and vitalizes the one artistic element closest to him in his environment, that ritual drama of courtly ceremony directed almost entirely toward the fam-ily tree and the sterile burial vaults of the Rosenmolds: an exaggerated classicism. (The Ancestors' Gallery at the Re-sidenz in Munich where Ludwig II grew up, a place Pater also would have understood as both like and unlike Marius's family mausoleum, contained 131 portraits of the crown prince's uniformly impressive forebears.) Young Duke Carl, having perceived a similarity of function between himself and Apollo, and having been told he resembled the god, first plays the Apollonian role in a proto-Wagnerian opera, *Bal-der*, then, by staging a mock funeral and reappearance, turns his life into a literal reenactment of the Apollo-Balder myth. This Germanic *Festspiel* is further literalized by Carl's actual death in his effort to bring Apollo with his lyre to Germany. He revives not in his own person but in the beautiful skating figure of Goethe fifty years later who, " 'like a son of the gods' " (153), seems the true Apollonian at last. As Conrad

Celtes's "Ode to Apollo" fathers Carl's enthusiasm for art, so Carl's struggle and sacrifice initiates the artistic patriotism that Lessing proclaimed and the return to nature of which Goethe was the herald. The concluding image of Goethe skating in his mother's furs expresses the inheritance of the past by the present, an image which anticipates that in *Gaston* of Montaigne enveloped in his father's mantle. Celtes, Carl, Goethe, Pater, "linking paternally, filially, age to age," are thus (to modulate from the paternal to the fraternal and adapt the myth of the Dioscuri) "ever coming and going, interchangeably, but [all] alike gifted now with immortal youth."

Of Pater's art generally, Arthur Symons observed: "It is all, the criticism, and the stories, and the writing about pictures and places, a confession, the *vraie vérité* . . . about the world in which he lived."[14] This Pater, glimpsed by his readers among the juxtaposed levels of theme, mood, and chronology—not only within *Imaginary Portraits* but in the whole range of his writing—is neither a directly autobiographical Oxford don leading an existence independent of his prose nor an objective mind criticizing art on its technical values, presenting arguments on their logical merits, keeping himself separate. One might say that Pater's presence is a sort of hidden text within or under the overt text, an "under-texture" (*Miscellaneous Studies*, 84), so to speak. Pater thus inserts himself into the texture of his language as the decentered object of its discourse, exactly as he had done by completing Marie-Marguerite's portrait, boldly raising criticism to the level of creation by aligning his avowed subject with himself.

14. Symons, *Figures*, p. 319.

# CHAPTER THREE

# Parent and Child

As a schoolboy aspiring to future fame, Pater considered the Latin meaning of his unusual name "a valuable asset"; and, Thomas Wright records, among the boys in his form there was also a Pope and an Abbot; the headmaster, "who called them his 'three fathers,' used to observe that it was a singular circumstance that in a form consisting of only a dozen boys three should be called 'father' in different languages." More recently, Michael Levey reports also that Pater's schoolfellows called him "Parson Pater" and "the Pater."[1] Now every father has offspring, not only the Victorian paterfamilias but even the Father of the Pater Noster. But though he is named a father, Pater neither knew his father (Richard Glode Pater died prematurely—significantly, the males in the family all died early—and afterward Walter could scarcely remember him) nor, being "all powerful in written word, impotent in life,"[2] had he a child—except the text.

To understand this motif of paternity as it relates to Pater's life and art, one must begin with the relation of father and son in his earliest and most explicitly autobiographical portrait. On one of those small scraps of paper on which he habitually composed notes to himself, Pater wrote: "Child in the House: voilà, the germinating, original, source, specimen, of all my *imaginative* work."[3] Reflecting as it does

---

1. Wright, *Pater*, 1: 87, 92–93; Levey, *The Case of Walter Pater* (London: Thames and Hudson, 1978), pp. 46, 64, 81.

2. Moore, *Avowals*, p. 214.

3. *Letters*, ed. Evans, p. xxix.

the paternal-filial relationship, "The Child in the House" is
indeed the source of Pater's imaginative, autobiographical
work. In the portrait, Pater's deceased father, depicted as a
soldier dead in India, becomes a ghostly presence the child
"hated" (*Miscellaneous Studies*, 191). This antagonism that
Florian-Pater initially feels toward the absent father is, typi-
cally, that sense of a broken wholeness, the absent godhead,
halves disjoined. Although the connection is not overtly
stated, certain militaristic-biblical figures (Joshua, Jacob,
Aaron, Moses) assume the paternal role and develop the idea
of the recovered father as the "sacred double" who is "at
once the reflex and the pattern" (194) of the child's nobler self.
In this recovery of his father within "sacred history" (193),
Florian anticipates Gaston's perception of the Latour family
record as "a second sacred history" (*Gaston*, 4).

"The Child in the House" closes with a symbolic death in
which the house appears to the child who has left it to be
"like the face of one dead" (*Miscellaneous Studies*, 196). The
house, like the sleepy ceremonies of Rosenmold or the ritual
of exhumation in Denys's story, is expressive of an outworn,
"dead" classical form which must be paternally rejuvenated.
The generations of ancestors laid away in the dusty family
mausoleum at White-nights represent Marius's own dead
heritage, but a heritage which the recovery of the father will
be able to revitalize. There in the mausoleum Marius the son
is symbolically buried with his mother ("this boy of his own
age had taken filial place beside her there, in his stead"), and
he becomes identified with his father: "That hard feeling,
again, which had always lingered in his mind with the
thought of the father he had scarcely known, melted wholly
away, as he read the precise number of his years, and reflected suddenly—He was of my own present age. . . . And
with that came a blinding rush of kindness, as if two alien-

ated friends had come to understand each other at last"
(*Marius,* 2: 206–07).

The textual nature of the recovery of this paternal figure is
significant. Sebastian van Storck's refusal to be painted or to
sign his letters reflects a rejection of the textual doppelgänger—a refusal to be caught "in a fragment of perfect expression" (1: 155). Only at the end does Sebastian reverse
his attitude, heroically losing his life to save a child, and
so manifest a belated paternity. But in "The Child in the
House," by contrast, the centrality of the text is affirmed
through the recovery of the father in the holy pictures of the
sacred book, an anticipation of the striking combination of
literary text and pictorial icon found later in Denys's manuscript of Ovid. So too, in Marius's ritual of death and rebirth,
the discovery of identity with his father comes through the
act of *reading* the inscription on his tomb. Fulfilling paternity
in his act of sacrifice, Marius discovers Cornelius to be
" 'More than brother!' . . . —'like a son also!' " through
whom he can possess the future "even as happy parents
reach out, and take possession of it, in and through the sur-
vival of their children" (2: 209–10). Further, Marius's paternity
and Cornelius's possession of futurity refer back to Pater's
role as autobiographer; for in the year *Marius* was published, 1885, Pater himself was, like Marius, "the precise
number of years" that his own father had been when, at age
forty-five, he had died.[4] As Marius and Pater attain the age at
which their respective fathers died, each in turn enacts a
ritual designed to father himself anew, Pater's act of writing
the novel becoming thereby, on the deepest level, the subject
of the autobiographical narrative itself. In producing his au-

4. Richard Pater's death, at age forty-five, is recorded on his death cer-
tificate as 28 January 1842. Pater, at the publication of *Marius* on 4 March
1885, was seven months into his forty-fifth year.

tobiography, re-creating his life textually, Pater becomes both a father and a son. He fathers the text, and yet that text is his own life, himself. Pater thereby becomes his own *pater*, compensating for the actual father he could scarcely remember.

Pater's loss of his father at the age of two and a half and his lifelong effort to regain the absent paternal presence belong to a larger pattern of psychological trauma. At the age of fourteen, Pater also unexpectedly lost his mother. So powerfully moved by the "many causes of sorrow inherent in the ideal of maternity, human or divine," Pater afterward even projected his childhood anguish onto a picture by Raphael's father, seeing in it "not the anticipated sorrow of the 'Mater Dolorosa' over the dead son, but the grief of a simple household over the mother herself taken early from it" (*Miscellaneous Studies*, 40). Although Maria Pater died at a moment when her son, not happy at school, must have especially needed her comfort, his dependence would have been balanced also by a desire for freedom. One recalls Marius's relief in the liberty afforded him by the death of his father whom he perceived as hard and stern; Pater as a very young child, but not so young as not to have felt an oedipal rivalry with the father for his mother's favors, may have perceived the sudden death of his father as a consequence of his own will. Of course, an ambiguity of feeling results: the removal of the rival is achieved, but guilt and an insatiable yearning for the absent father's love arise. Afterward, the mother's death suddenly constitutes this paradoxical condition of loss and gain as a pattern. Thomas Wright says that he had "proof" of the autobiographical origin of the incident connected with the death of Marius's mother. The angry gesture and slighting word of Marius at her departure for what was expected to be a routine visit was an actual event which Pater "never after called to mind without self-reproach."[5] As Pater arranged the incident, Marius avoids a great burden of remorse because his mother sent for him at the end and a reconciliation occurred. Wright does not mention this reconciliation as part of Pater's own experience; indeed, he implies the opposite. With or without this restored contact, the traumatic occurrence of a dreaded yet desired separation from parental dominance, exacerbated by a sense of power misused for destruction, created an indelible sense of guilt and remorse for having caused or willed her sudden death. Such an inference can be supported by an analysis of the overdetermined passages in Pater's writings which reveal his autobiographical fears and desires.

Probably Walter's mother, Maria, overshadowed by the more lively and loving Aunt Bessie, was less the dominant, devoted mother than a "languid and shadowy" (*Marius*, 1: 17) figure like the mother of Marius. Even so, Pater is undoubtedly projecting an idealized fantasy, as earlier he had in describing Leonardo's doting father, when in the novel he writes that young Marius "came to think of women's tears, of women's hands to lay one to rest, in death as in the sleep of childhood, as a sort of natural want. . . . And as his mother became to him the very type of maternity in things, its unfailing pity and protectiveness, and maternity itself the central type of all love;—so, that beautiful dwelling-place lent the reality of concrete outline to a peculiar ideal of home, which throughout the rest of his life he seemed, amid many distractions of spirit, to be ever seeking to regain" (1: 21–22). Somewhat closer to Pater's actual sense of maternity may be those rejected mistresses of noble and glorious but absent lovers, except for Leonardo's father, who give birth to the

5. Wright, *Pater*, 1: 74.

extraordinary love child (Dionysus, Hippolytus, Psyche's
Voluptas, Denys, Columbe's son, the English poet) or those
ambiguous, mythic mothers as Artemis and Demeter with
their fostering and destructive sides. But the most transpar-
ently autobiographical projection may well be given by Pater
in his essay on Botticelli. There he writes that Botticelli's
Madonnas "shrink from the pressure of the divine child, and
plead in unmistakable undertones for a warmer, lower humanity" (*Renaissance*, 60), a mother-son relationship which
seems undeniably a reflection of Pater's own sense of maternal experience. Figures aloof and estranged, Botticelli's
Madonnas have about them the wistfulness of those exiled
"angels who, in the revolt of Lucifer, were neither for
Jehovah nor for His enemies" (54).

The central passage, a description of the Uffizi *Madonna
del Magnificat,* is as follows:

> Her trouble is in the very caress of the mysterious
> child, whose gaze is always far from her, and who has
> already that sweet look of devotion which men have
> never been able altogether to love, and which still
> makes the born saint an object almost of suspicion to his
> earthly brethren. Once, indeed, he guides her hand to
> transcribe in a book the words of her exaltation, the
> *Ave,* and the *Magnificat,* and the *Gaude Maria,* and the
> young angels, glad to rouse her for a moment from her
> dejection, are eager to hold the inkhorn and to support
> the book. But the pen almost drops from her hand,
> and the high cold words have no meaning for her, and
> her true children are those others, among whom, in
> her rude home, the intolerable honour came to her,
> with that look of wistful inquiry on their irregular
> faces which you see in startled animals—gipsy chil-
> dren, such as those who, in Apennine villages, still

hold out their long brown arms to beg of you, but on
Sundays become *enfants du choeur,* with their thick
black hair nicely combed, and fair white linen on their
sunburnt throats. [57]

Pater has read into Botticelli's painting the predicament of a
commonplace mother, able neither to love her gifted child
(whose otherworldly look of devotion perhaps was dupli-
cated in the pietistic young Pater) nor even to fathom his
destiny. Although, significantly, the child himself encour-
ages the transcription of those words—the composition of
the scriptural text—which testify to the mother's supposed
beatific vision, feelings of inferiority threaten him in her
clear preference for that "warmer, lower humanity" of his
more active siblings. Whereas in *Marius* the idealized fantasy
omitted the rival brother(s) and allowed the mother's attention to be focused wholly on Marius himself, here in the description of Botticelli's Madonna the psychic overtones of
Pater's rivalry with William for the mother's affection come
to the fore. Indeed, the concluding lines of the description,
having forsaken Botticelli entirely, are located squarely
within the precincts of Pater's own sphere of adult experience, on those irresistible beggars of money—or of love. In
competition with this sensuous reality, even the Christ child
loses.

I observed earlier in *Pater's Portraits* that "it is possible
to see Marius' name as the masculine form of *Mary,* the sor-
rowing and questing Demeter of the Middle Ages."[6] To an-
chor that observation more firmly, one must note that Pater's
mother's name was also Mary—and in the Latin form of Botticelli's Madonna: *Maria* Pater. Also, not only does her mar-
ried name invoke the holy family (mother Maria and the

6. Gerald Monsman, *Pater's Portraits* (Baltimore: Johns Hopkins University Press, 1967), p. 74.

fathering presence, Pater), but the close equivalence of Maria-Marius (similar to Amis-Amile, Denys-Dionysus, Apollo-Apollyon, or such veiled doppelgängers as Florian-Flavian, Cecil-Cecilia, Apuleius-Aurelius, Gaston-Gabrielle, or even the alliterative Walter Pater) hints that the feminine has been elided with the masculine to create a figure that for Pater is a projection of both the maternal and paternal, as Marius's eventual identification with both mother and father at White-nights affirmed. Pater, orphaned child longing for the love of an absent father and a remote mother, and his mirrored opposite, Marius, the parental figure he himself has created, together dramatize that lost familial wholeness which only the textual dialectic between inner and outer levels of character and author can restore. As Marius lies dying, "the tablet of the mind white and smooth, for whatsoever divine fingers might choose to write there" (*Marius*, 2: 220), he waits for Pater in the next frame out to reconstitute his wholeness and is thus turned back upon the divine child of the Uffizi *Magnificat* who himself will write those words in a book that will bestow lasting glory upon the parent. The dying parent is replaced by the child who, through the power of the autobiographical text to re-create himself, has assumed the parental role. In this, the character within the work of fiction has become the author of the fiction he is in, the inner frame swallowing the outer, the work turning itself inside out.

The metamorphosis of the mother who seems first to destroy the child with a threatening sense of inferiority but who ultimately is herself totally subordinated to his reputation is akin to the dialectical transformations of Dionysus who is ultimately "both the hunter and the spoil" (*Greek Studies*, 79). That this vindication of the son involves an almost mythic measure of hostility and violence, as well as an enormous guilt, seems clear from a number of consid-

erations. For example, Pater was drawn to Charles Lamb not
only because he was the closest writer in temperament and
style that Pater had read; not only because Lamb, living with
his sister, was an inescapable double of Pater and his sis-
ter(s); but most darkly because Mary Lamb actually killed her
mother as Pater feared he himself had had the power to do as
a child. Charles's sister Mary was both a reflection of Pater's
mother (Mary-Maria) and a component of his own nature:
she is that murderous double which slays the mother and yet
as Mary (gentle as a lamb) *is* the mother herself. Pater, I
think, was struck by the same conflict of impulse and restraint in the Lambs' lives as in his; and toward the end of
his essay he explains Lamb's very Paterian languor as shock
at discovering himself to have survived a Greek tragedy: "In
his writing, as in his life, that quiet is not the low-flying of
one from the first drowsy by choice, and needing the prick of
some strong passion or worldly ambition, to stimulate him
into all the energy of which he is capable; but rather the
reaction of nature, after an escape from fate, dark and insane
as in old Greek tragedy, following upon which the sense of
mere relief becomes a kind of passion, as with one who,
having narrowly escaped earthquake or shipwreck, finds a
thing for grateful tears in just sitting quiet at home, under
the wall, till the end of days" (*Appreciations*, 121–22). In the
next and final paragraph of the essay, Pater recalls that at his
childhood home of Enfield, which the Lambs had left barely
a decade earlier, beneath the tame and humdrum "surface of
things" lie violent alternations of atmosphere—"nowhere is
there so much difference between rain and sunshine"—
perpetually transforming the place and the individual with
its "portent of storm in the rapid light on dome and bleached
stone steeples" (122–23). This atmospheric alternation has its
counterpart in the landscape of Denys's Auxerre, attractive
for its mixtures of mood "when the tide of light and distant

cloud is travelling quickly over it, when rain is not far off, and every touch of art or of time on its old building is defined in clear grey" (*Imaginary Portraits*, 51–52). Foreshadowing in Denys's portrait the ceaselessly interacting antinomies which destroy and renew, this alternation of rain and sun in the essay on Lamb, in the only directly personal recollection in the whole range of Pater's writings, implies that Lamb's memories have become Pater's fantasies, not of place alone but also of murderous circumstance.

Significantly, parricide occurs at the structural center of *Marius the Epicurean* in the chapter "Manly Amusement." And, within this chapter, at its exact center lies the sentence narrating the beginning of the amusing games: "The arena, decked and in order for the first scene, looked delightfully fresh" (*Marius*, 1: 236). Finally, at the center of the arena (L *harena, arena* sand, sandy place) and bespeaking that middle moment of destruction and renewal spread "certain great red patches" (1: 235). In what sense does a narrative that opens with the slaughter of the Ambarvalia and concludes with the slaughter of the Gallic Christians mean the reader to take this blood at the center? The sandy place with red patches has filiations with the image of blood in the essay on Prosper Mérimée also, both where "Colomba places in his hand the little chest which contains the father's shirt covered with great spots of blood" (*Miscellaneous Studies*, 25) and where Mérimée's style itself is likened to "some harshly dyed oriental carpet from the sumptuous floor of the Kremlin, on which blood had fallen" (18). Autobiographically, the patch of red goes back to one of Pater's earliest memories; Symons reports Pater's "terror of the train, and of 'the red flag, which meant blood.' "[7] There in the central chapter of *Marius* at the center of the arena is the blood on the sand, indicative of that terrifying, cruel, mystical moment in which one life is given

7. *Renaissance*, ed. Symons, p. xxii.

for another. In Pater's first translated story in *The Renaissance* (calling up comparison with the function of Apuleius's tale within the framework of *Marius*), he provides a variation on the myth of the Dioscuri in which the blood of the slain elder is given to "heal" the younger. This, the strongest image of blood in Pater's writings, occurs in the barbaric tale of Amis and Amile (*Renaissance*, 8–15, 27–29). Amis, the leper with the wife who would strangle him, correlates with the figure of Castor, the mortal subject to death, whereas Amile, together with his wife who weeps over Amis and yearns to heal him, correlates with the elder Polydeuces who can bestow the gift of life. Or, to shift from the fraternal to the parental and read the tale in terms of another mythic paradigm, the wives embody the opposing traits of Demeter's daughters or of Artemis who is not only "the assiduous nurse of children, and patroness of the young," but also the goddess of death (*Greek Studies*, 168, 170). Amile beheads his children to obtain blood for a ritual washing so that Amis might be restored to health. But the would-be destruction of the child by the parent turns out to be a vicarious sacrifice of the parent for the sake of his offspring. Echoing the returns of Polydeuces and Persephone, the culminating restoration of Amis to health is thus paralleled by the return of the children to life, he being an equivalent for them.

So too, in the amusing games, Artemis is present in the arena as "the symbolical expression of two allied yet contrasted elements of human temper and experience—man's amity, and also his enmity, towards the wild creatures, when they were still, in a certain sense, his brothers. She is the complete, and therefore highly complex, representative of a state, in which man was still much occupied with animals . . . as his equals, on friendly terms or the reverse,—a state full of primeval sympathies and antipathies, of rivalries and common wants" (*Marius*, 1: 237). The love-hate relationship

of the arena with its slaughter of the pregnant animals can be
seen to correspond to Pater's fantasy of slaying the mother in
the place of the child. In this, Pater the orphaned son numbers himself among the newborn creatures who escape "from
their mother's torn bosoms" (1: 238). This same image occurs
later in a slightly altered guise in the martyr Blandina whose
" 'whole body was torn asunder' " (2: 192). Her symbolic
maternity is attested to: " 'Last of all, the blessed Blandina
herself, as a mother that had given life to her children, and
sent them like conquerors to the great King, hastened to
them, with joy at the end, as to a marriage-feast; the enemy
himself confessing that no woman had ever borne pain so
manifold and great as hers' " (2: 195). That the young may be
enfranchised—albeit themselves sent to death but as the
conquerors of death—the mother must be rent.

The amity-enmity pattern of man toward his " 'younger
brothers' " (1: 237) autobiographically connects the scene
in the arena not only with mother-son relationships but also
with the sibling rivalry of William and Walter: "primeval
sympathies and antipathies, of rivalries and common
wants." Pater's older brother William filled the vacuum of
the absent father, becoming for him a surrogate father both
as a rival for the mother's affection and as an alter ego, an
idealized version of himself. Through William, the handsome, virile elder brother with military attainments, Pater
compensated for the acutely warped body image which at
one time or another caused him to conceal his mouth with an
enormous Bismarckian moustache and to caricature himself
both as a carp and, upon seeing his portrait, as a barbary
ape.[8] Perhaps at William's nearly fatal illness during the
composition of *Marius* and certainly at his death a few years
later, that old sense of triumph in the destruction of a rival

8. Wright, *Pater,* 1: 192–93; MacColl, "Pater," p. 760; William Rothen-
stein, *Men and Memories* (New York: Coward-McCann, 1931–40), 1: 155.

and the inevitable pangs of loss repeated themselves for the third time in Pater's life. Though there is no evidence, as Wright claims, that the brothers "had been to an extraordinary degree engrossed in each other"—quite the contrary, for no letters between them survive, and in one of Pater's rare mentions of William he complains of never being informed of his whereabouts—it is nonetheless probable that the blow of William's death "had been a crushing one."[9] Although this occurred when Pater was well beyond the middle of life, the preexisting pattern associated with the deaths of his father and mother called forth the same emotional response of guilt expressed in *Marius* when its hero confesses: " 'I find it hard to get rid of a sense that I, for one, have failed in love. I could yield to the humour till I seemed to have had my share in those great public cruelties, the shocking legal crimes which are on record. . . . To some, perhaps, the necessary conditions of my own life may cause me to be opposed, in a kind of natural conflict, regarding those interests which actually determine the happiness of theirs. I would that a stronger love might arise in my heart!' " (2: 177). Though Pater unconsciously sought in William the image of what he himself longed to be, he must have kept his brother at arm's length to avoid a sense of competition and envy. This approach and avoidance, aggression and guilt, working itself out over nearly a half century, is the hidden energizing inspiration of Pater's art. Long before his third bereavement, Pater had begun to exorcise this conflict in himself, sublimating or displacing his oedipal and sibling rivalries by an equivalent drama of the text. He was, in short, no longer helpless in dealing with death, a prey to unrestrained feelings of guilt and remorse.

In the chapter entitled "Euphuism," Pater speaks of "the burden of precedent, laid upon every artist" (1: 99), a theme

9. Wright, *Pater*, 2: 99; *Letters*, ed. Evans, p. 1.

connected with Marius's earlier yearning to be free from the
gods' and his father's control. Yet the desire to break free of
the burden of precedent leaves the writer with a sense of
guilt for "a sympathy and understanding broken, . . . the
thought of those averted or saddened faces grown suddenly
strange to us."[10] The way to "make it new" (as Ezra Pound
later exhorted) without suffering the constraint of having
alienated the past is simply to become the elder, the parent,
by reweaving in one's own art the elements of the past. As
Pater pointed out in *Plato*, the subject matter in any given
artistic artifact has all existed before; only the form is new.
Thus, in Cecilia's church the older pagan art was not destroyed by the newer Christian decorations but harmonized
in "the old way of true *Renaissance*—being indeed the way of
nature with her roses, the divine way with the body of man,
perhaps with his soul—conceiving the new organism by no
sudden and abrupt creation, but rather by the action of a new
principle upon elements, all of which had in truth already
lived and died many times" (2: 95–96). As the alienation of
Botticelli's Christ child is resolved by fathering the words in
the book, so also the birth of Pater as an artist corresponds to
his liberation from the past, from parental threats of inferiority or from literary precedent, by the assertion of his
own paternity through writing. The ostensible "aim at an
actual theatrical illusion" (1: 238) in the games of the arena
provides Pater with the perfect paradigm for the undermin-
ing of all those distinctions between parent and child, origin
and repetition, subject and object, author and reader, center
and margin. Thus, in contrast to the undeniable reality of the
spectators in the grandstands, the "scene" in the ring seems
illusory; but as in the stories of both Denys and Duke Carl,
the playacting turns out to be real. Pater perhaps had wit-

10. From the lecture, "Moral Philosophy," quoted in *Letters*, ed.
Evans, pp. xxv–vi.

nessed spectacles at Covent Garden or elsewhere; there the purpose would have been to create an illusion of reality, whereas at Rome the actual was made to seem merely staged. In the interplay between Rome and London, the opposition between center and margin becomes a perpetual turning back of the one upon the other so that in the world of the arena the question is perpetually open: which is the origin, the real? and which the repetition, the illusion? So, too, within the arena of the text there are no primordial, first parental figures to which the child need be subordinate. Pater becomes his own *pater* through a logic which prohibits the ontological determination of any one entity at the expense of the other.

Marcus Aurelius, who sponsors the bloodshed of "Manly Amusement," is the expression of an emerging modern mentality. The very fact that he patronizes so many deities and religions suggests a fragmentation not present in the simpler outlook of his subjects who march in the procession of Isis. Aurelius anticipates not only the medieval "fever dream" brought about by the "absence of the beloved"— that visible ideal of Zeus, Athena, or Isis—but also the modern return to the Heraclitean creed of the flux which began already in the age of faith with the loss of the visible ground. In his essay on Mérimée, Pater defined this modern predicament in terms wholly applicable to Aurelius: "Fundamental belief gone, in almost all of us, at least some relics of it remain—queries, echoes, reactions, after-thoughts; and they help to make an atmosphere, a mental atmosphere, hazy perhaps, yet with many secrets of soothing light and shade, associating more definite objects to each other by a perspective pleasant to the inward eye against a hopefully receding background of remoter and ever remoter possibilities" (*Miscellaneous Studies*, 15). This "receding background" of "ever remoter possibilities" is a kind of reflexivity which mirrors emptiness: "Mirror on mirror mirrored is all the show," as W. B. Yeats in a very Paterian poem ("The Statues") later described the condition. Thus, for Aurelius in his empty palace, the ideal city of mankind is but a hazy and remote image:

> it had been actually, in his clearest vision of it, a con-fused place, . . . haunted by strange faces, whose novel expression he, the great physiognomist, could by no means read. Plato, indeed, had been able to ar-ticulate, to see, at least in thought, his ideal city. But just because Aurelius had passed beyond Plato, in the scope of the gracious charities he pre-supposed there, he had been unable really to track his way about it. Ah! after all, according to Plato himself, all vision was but reminiscence, and this, his heart's desire, no place his soul could ever have visited in any region of the old world's achievements. He had but divined, by a kind of generosity of spirit, the void place, which another experience than his must fill. [*Marius*, 2: 40]

Duke Carl's aspiration to be propelled out of space into fu-ture time suggests the same yearning for an absent reality.

What fills that empty reflexivity is a sympathy with the concerns of others, an insight Pater perhaps derived in part from Goethe. Pater describes the essence of Pico della Mirandola's humanism, and surely his own also, as "that belief of which he seems never to have doubted, that nothing which has ever interested living men and women can wholly lose its vitality—no language they have spoken, nor oracle beside which they have hushed their voices, no dream which has once been entertained by actual human minds, nothing about which they have ever been passionate, or expended time and zeal" (*Renaissance*, 49). Even though in one sense

Aurelius may have "passed beyond" Plato, yet Plato by sympathy had been able to fill that "void place" with a living plenitude. His genius, Pater writes, is that of one

> who is become a lover of the invisible, but still a lover, and therefore, literally, a seer, of it, carrying an elaborate cultivation of the bodily senses . . . into the world of intellectual abstractions, . . . filling that "hollow land" with delightful colour and form, as if now at last the mind were veritably dealing with . . . living people who play upon us through the affinities . . . of *persons*: . . . —There, is the formula of Plato's genius. . . . No one perhaps has with equal power literally sounded the unseen depths of thought, and, with what may be truly called "substantial" word and phrase, given locality there to the mere adumbrations, the dim hints and surmise, of the speculative mind. [*Plato*, 139–40]

But ultimately Plato, too, is frustrated in his vision of the City of the Perfect; and to some he seems, rather sadly, to be "a mind trying to feed itself on its own emptiness" (143).

In a letter to Mrs. Humphry Ward, Pater indicated that the "historic church" itself might constitute a possible ideal: "To my mind, the beliefs, and the function in the world, of the historic church, form just one of those obscure but all-important possibilities, which the human mind is powerless effectively to dismiss from itself; and might wisely accept, in the first place, as a workable hypothesis."[11] Yet in large measure even religion has lost its grip on an objective and solid reality: "Quite in the way of one who handles the older sorceries, the Church has a thousand charms to make the absent near. Like the woman in the idyll of Theocritus—' . . . draw to my house the man I love,' is the cry of all her bizarre

11. *Letters*, ed. Evans, p. 64.

rites."[12] Although antedating the letter to Mrs. Ward by
nearly two decades and differing sharply in tone, the por-
trayal of the church as a mistress attempting to draw back
through sorcery the lover who has deserted her is not unlike
its description as a provider of those "obscure but all-
important possibilities" that lie between a vision and a void:
in both characterizations there is an absence which reaches
out for a presence. The comparison to the woman in Theocritus's second idyll aligns the church with Pater's typical
female figure—with the deserted Psyche, for example. But
Psyche regains her absent Cupid not by the sorcery of direct
vision (her original error) but indirectly in the form of her
child to be born: " 'in the face of this little child, at the least,
shall I apprehend thine' " (*Marius*, 1: 93). By turning her
vanished old love back upon the new, Psyche summons her
absent lord.

Psyche's ability to confront that regressus ad infinitum of
"ever remoter possibilities" and employ it against itself to
invoke the absent ground is derived from her power of
sympathy—"a perfect imaginative love, centered upon a
type of beauty entirely flawless and clean" (1: 92). Thus
Marius writes in his journal: " 'the only principle, perhaps,
to which we may always safely trust is a ready sympathy
with the pain one actually sees. . . . The future will be with
those who have the most of it; while for the present, as I
persuade myself, those who have much of it, have something
to hold by, even in the dissolution of self, which is, for every
one, no less than the dissolution of the world it represents for
him' " (2: 183). The bloodshed of the arena is merely a
meaningless slaughter for those who without sympathy per-
petrate it. The moral "blindness" (1: 242) of the emperor to

12. Pater, "Poems by William Morris," p. 302. The translation here sub-
stituted for the Greek of Pater's quotation is taken from *Theocritus*, ed. and
trans. A. F. S. Gow (Cambridge: Cambridge University Press, 1953), 1: 17.

the cruelty of the games in the arena and his solipsistic isolation in an empty and nearly windowless house contrast ironically with Marius's sense of dissolving prison walls by which he escapes from himself and identifies the external world as no longer foreign but as that in which his life consists. Just as Plato the seer had a sense of the dialectic between self and Other being held together by "the affinities, the repulsion and attraction, of *persons*" (*Plato*, 140), so Marius comes to sense the reality of "the hypothesis of an eternal friend to man, just hidden behind the veil of a mechanical and material order, but only just behind it, ready perhaps even now to break through" (*Marius*, 2: 63–64). Here Marius comes to terms with alterity and fills that void before which Aurelius stopped by naming it a kindred spirit.

The image of blood upon the sand is given its most consoling restatement in Marius's ritual of burial at White-nights. There, in an act of sympathy for the kindred Other, he consigns his ancestors' ashes to the earth, reflexively turning the dead back upon the fruitful womb of life. At the time at which he would have been formulating this description of Marius's ritual at White-nights, Pater was at work also on "Sir Thomas Browne" (composed in 1883, as dated by Pater's reading lists). Pater there speaks of Browne's "awe-stricken sympathy with those, whose bones 'lie at the mercies of the living' " and tells the story of Pope Gregory who, having been "requested by certain eminent persons to send them some of those relics he sought for so devoutly in all the lurking-places of old Rome, took up, it is said, a portion of common earth, and delivered it to the messengers; and, on their expressing surprise at such a gift, pressed the earth together in his hand, whereupon the sacred blood of the Martyrs was beheld flowing out between his fingers" (*Appreciations*, 157). In like manner, Pater attributed to Wordsworth's religion of nature a sense of voices coming

from low walls, green mounds, and even half-obliterated
epitaphs:

> Religious sentiment, consecrating the affections and
> natural regrets of the human heart, above all, that pit-
> iful awe and care for the perishing human clay, of
> which relic-worship is but the corruption, has always
> had much to do with localities, with the thoughts
> which attach themselves to actual scenes and places.
> Now what is true of it everywhere, is truest of it in
> those secluded valleys where one generation after
> another maintains the same abiding-place; and it was
> on this side, that Wordsworth apprehended religion
> most strongly. Consisting, as it did so much, in the
> recognition of local sanctities, in the habit of con-
> necting the stones and trees of a particular spot of
> earth with the great events of life, till the low walls,
> the green mounds, the half-obliterated epitaphs
> seemed full of voices, and a sort of natural oracles, the
> very religion of these people of the dales appeared but
> as another link between them and the earth, and was
> literally a religion of nature. [49–50]

That sense of an "eternal friend" just hidden behind a "material order" coalesces with a sense of multiple generations in
one locality—of blood, of voices within the earth—to become finally the accomplished goal of Marius's ritual at
White-nights: "Dead, yet sentient and caressing hands
seemed to reach out of the ground and to be clinging about
him" (*Marius*, 2: 208).

The limitation of Aurelius in the face of diminished possibilities is evidenced by his inability to conceive of the earth
after the fashion of Marius, ironically confirmed in the moment of his greatest triumph. Pater remarks that Aurelius's
Justus Triumphus, which occurs as a prelude to Marius's re-

turn to White-nights, has been sanctioned by the "blood-shed" of "our own ancestor" (2: 197). This aligns against ancient Rome both Pater's readers and also Marius who, upon hearing of the slaughter of the Gallic Christians, dis-covers within himself a growing disaffection. In contrast to his home, which Marius visits at the end of this penulti-mate chapter, the German's house has been taken off the earth and is carried in the triumphal procession on a framework. This enforced isolation from the soil (as again with the spiteful burning of the martyrs' bodies) is indicative of Aurelius's deeper failure to turn shed blood back upon the womb of earth. And such apparent sympathy as Aurelius does manifest cannot get beyond a barren reflexivity and achieve specularity. Himself without a natural father and adopted, he adopts the children of Cassius whom he has killed. Analogously, that "marvellous but malign beauty," the "unquiet, dead goddess" (2: 202) Faustina, shelters girl orphans under her rubric of "the 'Faustinian Children' " (2: 203). But in contrast with Blandina in the previous chapter (whose name is associated with one of Pater's favorite adjec-tives, *bland,* suggestive of harmony and calm), Faustina does not stand in a mutually regenerative relationship with her children. Both Aurelius and Faustina contrast with the pa-triarchal peace—blandness, if you will—of the preceding generation of Antonius Pius, in which the old emperor's "hands red at vintage-time with the juice of the grapes" (2: 202) foreshadow the more sinister bloodshed of Aurelius and the "stain" (2: 202) of Faustina's immorality.

Unlike Aurelius, Marius is without tangible family but nevertheless achieves a true familial relationship. Returning frequently to the church in Cecilia's house, he witnesses on one occasion her burial of a child: "Dead children, children's graves—Marius had been always half aware of an old superstitious fancy in his mind concerning them; as if in

coming near them he came near the failure of some lately-
born hope or purpose of his own" (2: 188). Marius's "lately-
born hope" had been for a marriage with Cecilia, in whom
his "long-cherished desires" (2: 187) for a family had been
given momentary encouragement. But the rule against second marriages for widows of ordained spouses links itself
with the strongly Pauline cast of his sentiments to suggest
the incompatibility for him of flesh and spirit. Like Lamb's
(or Pater's) renunciation of the " 'feverish, romantic tie of
love' " (*Appreciations*, 108), Marius aspires to a filial or
brotherly relation free from "random affections" (*Marius*, 2:
187; "random passions" in earlier editions). Marius realizes
he has reached one sort of emotional dead end—"he felt that
he too had had to-day his funeral of a little child" (2:
188)—but instinctively aware of the possibility for nonphysi-
cal familial relationships, he turns his lost desire back upon a
new hope for the future through the Christian burial of a
child (symbol of his failed hopes given new life) which had
died at White-nights at about that moment of transition from
the pre-Christian to the Christian era. A falling fragment had
chipped "a minute coffin of stone, and the fracture had revealed a piteous spectacle of the mouldering, unburned
remains within; the bones of a child, as he understood, which
might have died, in ripe age, three times over, since it
slipped away from among his great-grandfathers, so far up
in the line" (2: 206). Like the shrunken exhumed saint in
"Denys l'Auxerrois," this unburied ancestral child cannot
be newborn, nor can the aspirations of Marius and his forebears be vitalized, until it is returned to the regenerative
womb of the earth.

The growth, decay, and renewal of the earth in its
changes and the associated myths of the Dioscuri, Semele,
Hyacinthus, Demeter, and Dionysus not only lie behind the
narrative action of *Marius* but also allow this dramatic pattern

to be interpreted as an allegory of textual composition. By surrendering his quotidian life to the autobiographical text so that the cultural heritage may be regenerated, Pater as author repeats Marius's ritual of returning the dead child to the womb of the earth—a ritual that precipitated the cataclysmic denouement of the earthquake and signified the rending that precedes new life. Just as the young animals escape from the torn wombs of the pregnant mothers in the arena, so preexisting works of literature are torn (like the "tearing open" of the hillside by lightning)[13] in order that, rewoven by Pater, he may be liberated from precedent—not by here being orphaned like the animals but by an attainment of paternity through composition. Thus, when Pater remarks of Marius's burial of his ancestors "that he determined to bury all that, deep below the surface, to be remembered only by him, and in a way which would claim no sentiment from the indifferent" (2: 207), Pater is really describing the textual reflexivity of his own life. Unlike direct confessions, indirect autobiography does not reveal its subject to the casual reader of "the surface" (*sur-* + *face:* the form or face above); its subject partakes, rather, of "the *hiddenness of perfect things*" (1: 93), not unlike the face of the child of Psyche about to be born. " 'Tis art's function to conceal itself" (1: 97) may have been quoted by Pater to mean not only art's hidden labor but also its deepest autobiographical lineaments. The absent or veiled form—that face which persists beneath the perpetual alternations of life and death—can be reconstituted not by some exhumation (by any direct autobiographical revelation) but by being born anew from the earth—born anew from that metaphysical "ground" of all being in the next frame out, the cultural heritage of words.

Only by "a generous loan of one's self" (*Imaginary Portraits*, 145) can an author through a reflexive autobio-

13. Pater, "Romanticism," p. 66.

graphical structure turn the moribund subject back upon a regenerative life. By arranging Aurelius's writings (as the bones of Marius's ancestors at White-nights or the artifacts of the pagan past in Cecilia's house had been rearranged), a life is almost spontaneously uncovered beneath the "dry surface" of dreary statistical fact and debris: "Marius now discovered, almost as if by accident, below the dry surface of the manuscripts entrusted to him . . . reflections upon what was passing, . . . conversations with the reader . . . and . . . morsels of his conversation with himself. It was the romance of a soul (to be traced only in hints, wayside notes, quotations from older masters), as it were in lifelong, and often baffled search after some vanished or elusive golden fleece, or Hesperidean fruit-trees, or some mysterious light of doctrine, ever retreating before him" (*Marius*, 2: 45–46). It is as if Aurelius the modernist were in pursuit of Isis, but an Isis who now moves against a "receding background" of "ever remoter possibilities" in which the emperor, lost in a metaphysical "void" in his empty palace, finds himself "unable really to track his way about." But just as the ancestral past is renewed in the earth, so Aurelius's absent wholeness can be regained in the continuity and duration of the reflexive text. Like the emperor Aurelius, Pico della Mirandola also remains "alive in the grave" of his "forgotten books" (*Renaissance*, 49, 48), owing to such sympathetic interpretations of his thought as Pater's, "generously expanding it"—as Pater says of Gaston's reading of Ronsard's poetry—"to the full measure of its intention" (*Gaston*, 55). This generous expansion is the same as the "generous loan of one's self"—a well-bred liberality of spirit but also a regenerative (L *gener-*, *genus* birth, family, fr. *gignere* to beget) or procreative act.

That any vitality in the predecessor waits upon this essentially critical effort of the aftercomer is clearly illustrated in the textual history of Fronto's correspondence with Aurelius: "a strange piece of literary good fortune, at the beginning of the present century, has set free the long-buried fragrance of this famous friendship of the old world, from below a valueless later manuscript" (*Marius*, 1: 223–24). In the same manner that nineteenth-century editorial solicitude sets "free the long-buried" friendship, so "in the year 1780, the long-lost text of the Homeric Hymn to Demeter was discovered among the manuscripts of the imperial library at Moscow; and, in our own generation, the tact of an eminent student of Greek art, Sir Charles Newton, has restored to the world the buried treasures of the little temple and precinct of Demeter, at Cnidus" (*Greek Studies*, 82). Although with the recovery of the Homeric Hymn "portions of the text are missing" (83), Pater proceeds to give an abbreviated translation in which the "long-lost text" is reconstituted with no sense of its missing parts. Moscow's "lost" text or the "buried" letters of Fronto and the artifacts of Demeter have their mythic counterparts in Polydeuces' lost brother Castor or in Demeter's daughter of the underworld, Persephone (who also is the subject of the long-lost text): each is brought back with something of the excitement of a return to life.

This reflexive freeing or opening up of a relationship between old and new is present even in Marius's first entering his family's mausoleum. Surrounded by tall poplars like Persephone's moldering palace of death (94), the mausoleum has its door forced outward to free the dead from their underworld isolation and to begin the regenerative cycle of nature. As he stands "in the place which had been so often in his thoughts" (*Marius*, 2: 205), Marius puts himself literally in a previously mental place, imaginary and actual changing position in concert with old and new. So also, in the impressive final movement of Pater's narrative, Marius himself awaits a metamorphosis. As he lies dying, Marius recalls to mind his lifelong "purpose of preparing himself towards possible further revelation some day—towards some ampler vision, which should take up into itself and explain this world's delightful shows, as the scattered fragments of a poetry, till then but half-understood, might be taken up into the text of a lost epic, recovered at last" (2: 219–20). Like the lost Homeric Hymn or the image of Zeus fragmented into a thousand reflections, the Ur-text has been scattered or hidden beneath the surface flux and can be returned to its former wholeness only through that perpetual interplay in which all differential relations of real and imaginary, old and new, life and death, are grounded. In effect, Marius, "the tablet of the mind white and smooth," is awaiting that act of critical recomposition in the next frame out to do for him what he had done for Aurelius; that is, turn his imaginary being back upon the real and, by "whatsoever divine fingers might choose to write," give him life.

This motif of rebirth through change of form had been invoked, for example, at the exact structural center of each chapter in the diptych, "Two Curious Houses": on the one hand, in the pagan belief in the power of the gods "to refashion the form of a woman into that of a bird" (2: 83) as described in the legend of the Halcyon and, on the other, in the Christian act of burial which held "that these 'handfuls of white dust' would hereafter recompose themselves once more into exulting human creatures" (2: 100). But the price to be paid for this transformation, as the middle moment of the arena makes clear, is that of blood; for those "untranslatable" "ultimate differences" (*Renaissance*, 133) between the dialectical poles of experience can be spanned only by its shedding. Thus in Cecilia's house the roses and older pagan art can be "arranged and harmonised" (*Marius,* 2: 95) only by the exactment made evident in the *Epistle of the Churches of Lyons and Vienne:* bloodshed, martydom. In the final chapter, the martyr Hyacinthus, "whose blood had

stained the soil" (2: 210), together with the events of Marius's
arrest when "the earth had been stained afresh with the
blood of the martyrs Felix and Faustinus" (2: 211) bring the
bloodshed of the arena and the death of Marius into con-
junction. The name, Hyacinthus, directs attention to the old
myth of the hyacinth flower which grew from the blood of
the dying lad, its petals being inscribed with the signature
AI, meaning *woe.* But Marius initially fears that "from the
drops of his blood there would spring no miraculous, poetic
flowers" (2: 214) until he attains "the attitude of mind, to
which something higher than he, yet akin to him, would be
likely to reveal itself" (2: 220). Implied here in blood becoming the inscribed flower is the theme of the reconstitution of
the self in "poetic" or textual terms. Like ink on the paper,
blood on the sand signifies a trans*form*ation, a change in
*form* of the persisting and enduring elements renewed like
the roses (those "poetic flowers") in Cecilia's house. As the
middle term among all the differential relations, blood upon
the earth is the final image *in* Pater's art *of* his art. In the
arena of the text, all is dialectic, metamorphosis, flux. All of it
is blood on the sand—shed in hate, shed in love, shed in
perpetuity.

# CHAPTER FOUR

# The Abandoned Text

Although one could never argue that as an artistic achievement the unfinished *Gaston* has been considered as significant a work as *Marius*, its individual scenes and intricately
reflexive structure can be shown to be as masterfully planned
as those of its predecessor. In comparison with *Marius*,
*Gaston* exhibits a noticeable change in atmosphere: the violence is no longer quite so hidden under a tranquil surface,
and the ambiguity of motives, the personal regrets, and especially an abiding sense of guilt are all more prominent. Yet
what primarily distinguishes *Gaston* from *Marius* is Pater's
failure, despite repeated efforts, to finish it; and the deduc-
ible reasons are pertinent to an understanding of Pater's art
generally. In order to explain why *Gaston* was still largely
unfinished at Pater's death in 1894, it is necessary first to turn
one's attention to its structure and to the psychological
urgencies that build up within it.

Pater had begun work on *Gaston* shortly after or possibly
even before finishing *Marius*. The first five chapters appeared serially in *Macmillan's Magazine* from June to October
of 1888, and one additional chapter (entitled "Giordano
Bruno. Paris: 1586") came out as an independent article in the
*Fortnightly Review* for August 1889. After Pater's death, C. L.
Shadwell edited the six published chapters (the Bruno essay
had been revised by Pater for inclusion in *Gaston*) and one
new chapter from unpublished drafts. As projected by the
overly fastidious Shadwell (who withheld considerable ma-

terial as insufficiently polished), *Gaston* would seem to be a
rival to the love elegies of Sir Benjamin Backbite, envisioned
by their author "on a beautiful quarto page, where a neat
rivulet of text shall meander through a meadow of margin."[1]
Conjectures as to why the novel remained unfinished have
pointed variously to problems with characterization or with
the historical setting or with Pater's own frenetic schedule.[2]
As to characterization, it is suggested that either Pater lost
interest in his hero or that certain embarrassing emotional
themes cropped up (homosexuality, sadism) thwarting the
completion of his scheme for Gaston and others. The second
supposition alleges that the scope of the work with its complex historical background was just too broad to be distilled
fictionally; and with a post-Reformation setting, Pater could
not have solved quite so deftly as in *Marius* the problem of a
theologically reasoned assent. Finally, other critics suggest
that Pater began serialization of the work prematurely and
that in the light of his other commitments he overestimated
his ability to compose a chapter a month. Admittedly, all of
these factors may have contributed in some degree to his
faltering pace in 1888, but they do not account for his failure
to finish in the 1890s.

1. Richard Brinsley Sheridan, *The School for Scandal*, act 1, scene 1. Were
one to speculate as to *Gaston*'s length and form, one might guess that Pater
planned four books, as in *Marius*. Assuming six chapters in a book, the
Bruno chapter (retitled "The Lower Pantheism") would probably pick up the
story fourteen years later, beginning Part the Second; and Part the Third
would commence with the unpublished "Mi-Carême" (in fact labeled as
"Book Three: Chapter XIII"). The printed portion together with the unpublished material and its lacunae make *Gaston* about one-half the length of
*Marius* (although Herbert Horne, who tended to be accurate, noted that
Pater planned a *longer* work than *Marius*).

2. See, e.g., Teodor de Wyzewa, *Ecrivains étrangers*, 2nd ser. (Paris: Per-
rin, 1897), p. 267; A. C. Benson, *Walter Pater* (New York: Macmillan, 1906),
pp. 92, 140–47; d'Hangest, *Pater*, 2: 130–36, 320, 363; Gordon McKenzie, *The
Literary Character of Walter Pater* (Berkeley and Los Angeles: University of
California Press, 1967), p. 97; *Letters*, ed. Evans, p. xxxi.

Although Shadwell presumably had little detailed knowledge of motives when he conjectured that Pater became "dissatisfied with the framework which he had begun, and . . .
deliberately abandoned it" (*Gaston,* vi), this opinion is supported by the *Athenaeum* reviewer (T. Bailey Saunders) who
writes of *Gaston*: "Only a part of it had been given to the
world; and that part—with which, as Mr. Shadwell suggests,
and as the present writer can from his own knowledge
affirm, Pater was dissatisfied—had been deliberately abandoned, or rather, perhaps, put aside for future reconsidera-
tion."[3] The Shadwell-Saunders "dissatisfied" does not quite
suggest simple overcommitment, indicating that the mere
press of having to meet serial deadlines did not alone contrib-
ute to the termination of its run. The agonizingly slow pace
of composition after 1888 indicates a more basic thematic or
structural problem. Arthur Symons reported that in 1889
Pater thought he needed two or three years to finish; and in
1890 Herbert Horne told "Michael Field" that Pater had announced to him his intention of sacrificing his vacations in
order to complete the novel.[4] As Pater's library borrowings
indicate, he seems to have been actively researching the
historical background as late as the spring of 1893 when, for
the seventh time, he borrowed volumes of Pierre de Brantôme's works from the Taylorian Institution.

Doubtless the fact that Pater intended *Gaston* to be second
in a trilogy of which *Marius* had been the first accounts in
large measure for his selecting the complex age of the Valois
for its setting. As *Marius* had been set in the period of transition from paganism to Christianity, so *Gaston* is located in
the time just following the Reformation, in the transition

3. Review of *Gaston de Latour, Athenaeum,* 17 October 1896, p. 518.
4. Symons, *Figures,* p. 331; *Works and Days: From the Journal of Michael Field,* ed. T. and D. C. Sturge Moore (London: Murray, 1933), p. 119.

from Catholicism to Protestantism. Though the sixteenth century in France was an age of crisis, Pater focuses on history as filtered by memory and emotions, dissolving the action so radically that Gaston seems merely to have read about what happened all around him. In *Marius*, the thread of personal narrative is strongest in the closing chapters (book 4), although the use of Marius's journal in the place of direct dialogue still mutes his dramatic presence. Gaston as a dramatic figure may be only marginally more shadowy than Marius, but most readers will feel that the thread of narrative in *Gaston* is strongest in the *opening* chapters and is retained still in the first of the three finished portraits (that of Ronsard) but that it reappears only rarely in the essay on Montaigne and disappears entirely in the chapter on Bruno. In the chapter with the greatest potential for dramatic action, the penultimate "Shadows of Events," Pater dissolves the drama (marriage, betrayal, massacre, escape, childbirth) by a kind of retrospective distancing or temporal blurring of word and deed. The unpublished chapters carry forward the narrative thread only minimally. For example, nearly the whole of chapter 9 takes place within the single moment of Gaston's ascent of the staircase leading to the boudoir of Queen Margot; and in chapter 11 Pater apologizes for dwelling "at length on what was visible in Paris just then, on the mere historic scene there, forgetful it might seem of the company of Gaston, but only because I do suppose him thoughtfully looking on with us all the while, as essentially a creature of the eye, even more likely than others to be shaped by what he sees."[5] This emphasis upon the protagonist's processes of

5. Quoted in d'Hangest, *Pater*, 2: 365 n. 20. Although d'Hangest describes the unpublished chapters, I wish to thank John Sparrow, former warden of All Souls College, Oxford, for allowing me to study firsthand *Gaston*'s unpublished portions.

perception and the personification of culture, rather than upon the direct imitation of life, is central to the novel's artistic self-consciousness.

Pater's Gaston begins as a rather conventional Victorian lad, a "romantic" type questing for a spiritual home within the tangible world of the senses, for an ideal not in opposition to the actual but in harmony with it: "Two worlds, two antagonistic ideals, were in evidence before him. Could a third condition supervene, to mend their discord, or only vex him perhaps, from time to time, with efforts towards an impossible adjustment?" (*Gaston*, 38–39). And again: "Was there perhaps somewhere, in some penetrative mind in this age of novelties, some scheme of truth, some science about men and things, which might harmonise for him his earlier and later preference, 'the sacred and the profane loves,' or, failing that, establish, to his pacification, the exclusive supremacy of the latter?" (72). Like his fellow countryman du Bellay, of whom Pater had written in *The Renaissance*, Gaston is a dreamer longing for the harmonies of the unfallen world of childhood. His birthplace, the old château of Deux-manoirs, embodies in the unusual doubleness of its plan the attachment of brothers who did not want to be separated by their marriages.[6] This fraternal affection recalls Pater's description of its earlier French example, the friendship of Amis and Amile. There Pater had commented on "that curious interest of the *Doppelgänger*, which begins among the stars with the Dioscuri" (*Renaissance*, 9). Young Gaston's tranquil home, embodying the fraternal unity of self and Other, is not unlike

6. Pater's friend, Mrs. Mark Pattison, described as follows the château of Azay le Rideau—which the Paters had visited in 1877—in "French Châteaux of the Renaissance," *Contemporary Review* 30 (1877): 591: "It is built on two sides of a square, one side of which is prolonged somewhat and then abruptly truncated at an outward angle. This unsymmetrical ground plan is a trace still retained of earlier days, which are also faintly recalled by the elegant tourelles, carried on corbels, which complete each angle."

Marius's White-nights or Hippolytus's Eleusis—a world
ideally balanced between sense and spirit, not yet lapsed
into either impassioned sensuality or cold formalism. But if
childhood enjoys a perfect rapport between the self and the
sensuous world, "inward and outward being woven through
and through each other into one inextricable texture" (*Miscellaneous Studies*, 173), maturation, on the other hand, reveals an emphatically decentered identity: "that continual
vanishing away, that strange, perpetual weaving and unweaving of ourselves" (*Renaissance*, 236). Gaston's problem,
specifically, is the emerging spirit of relativism, expressed
for him in the Renaissance by Montaigne's or Bruno's
teachings and for Pater in the nineteenth century by Darwin,
Mill, and Spencer.

Yet, for a time at least, Gaston's "simple old-fashioned
faith, was blent harmoniously" with the desire of beauty,
"two neighbourly apprehensions of a single ideal" (*Gaston*,
22–23). Within this harmonious framework young Gaston
assumes clerk's orders in the family chapel of Saint Hubert.
Although it is a step which seemingly will end the race of
Latour, Gaston being the last of his line like Marius, Duke
Carl, or Sebastian van Storck, yet it is an act which testifies to
a belief in relationships that transcend the physical family. In
a passage that recalls Pater's earlier "purpurei panni" (the
phrase is Wilde's), Pater juxtaposes the warm, sunny landscape of La Beauce with the cool, shadowy interior of Saint
Hubert's, suggesting that the lad Gaston fuses outward sense
and inner vision:

Yes! there was the sheep astray, *sicut ovis quae
periit*—the physical world; with its lusty ministers, at
work, or sleeping for a while amid the stubble, their
faces upturned to the August sun—the world so im-
portunately visible, intruding a little way, with its

floating odours, in that semicircle of heat across the
old over-written pavement at the great open door,
upon the mysteries within. Seen from the incense-
laden sanctuary, where the bishop was assuming one
by one the pontifical ornaments, La Beauce, like a
many-coloured carpet spread under the great dome,
with the white double house-front quivering afar
through the heat, though it looked as if you might
touch with the hand its distant spaces, was for a moment the unreal thing. Gaston alone, with all his mystic preoccupations, by the privilege of youth, seemed
to belong to both, and link the visionary company
about him to the external scene. [10]

Like the impressionistic painter's initial dissociation of pure
color tones which recompose in the eye of the beholder only
at a distance, the colors and shapes of La Beauce are rendered
by Pater with pictorial richness. Pater's statement in "Giorgione" that a great picture in its primary aspect "has no more
definite message for us than an accidental play of sunlight
and shadow for a few moments on the wall or floor: is itself,
in truth, a space of such fallen light, caught as the colours are
in an Eastern carpet, but refined upon, and dealt with more
subtly and exquisitely than by nature itself" (*Renaissance,*
133) finds here its descriptive equivalent.

    That outer world of La Beauce, so like the impressions of
the perpetual flux described in the Conclusion to *The
Renaissance*—"unstable, flickering, inconsistent" (235)—is
seen "intruding a little way" through "the great open door"
toward the mysterious interior of the church. The open door
forcefully recalls such other visionary moments as Florian's
encounter through the open garden gate with the hawthorn
and its summer perfume. The "quivering" unreality of La
Beauce encircling the "incense-laden sanctuary" constitutes

Gaston within Saint Hubert's after the fashion of the human image described in the Conclusion: "a design in a web, the actual threads of which pass out beyond it" (234). Here the "web"—Mona Lisa, elsewhere, had "trafficked for strange webs with Eastern merchants" (125)—is a carpet, an image which turns us back to the eastern carpet in "Giorgione." And in the "many-coloured carpet" of La Beauce, the design of the child in the church is confirmed as the scenic center by the dramatic foreshortening which makes it seem "as if you might touch with the hand" the distant spaces of the landscape. (Much the same foreshortening occurred, for much the same reason, in Marius's vision at the shrine of Aesculapius where, looking through a cunningly contrived panel, he supposed he saw "Pisa.—Or Rome, was it? asked Marius, ready to believe the utmost in his excitement" [*Marius*, 1: 40].) In this context it is not without significance that another Gaston de Latour had undergone a similar ritual a century before: the flux which continuously modulates toward new centers has now again reconstituted the religious center, reanimated the past. Further, a heritage not physical only but also spiritual is manifest in "the old over-written pavement at the great open door," anticipating a similar image of continuity for Emerald Uthwart at school, who sits "at the heavy old desks, carved this way and that, crowded as an old churchyard with forgotten names" (*Miscellaneous Studies*, 207).

Although the doubleness of Deux-manoirs echoes Gaston's harmonious balance of inner and outer worlds— faith and beauty—yet on occasion certain "inward oppositions," even in his idyllic world of childhood, "beset him" (*Gaston*, 25). The condition of fraternal unity, expressed by the brothers Latour and later echoed for Gaston in Montaigne's friendship with the "incomparable" Etienne de la Boetie (" 'We were halves throughout, so that methinks by outliving him I defraud him of his part. I was so grown to be always his double in all things that methinks I am no more than half of myself' " [99]), must ultimately become for Gaston a thing of the past. Even before he leaves home, the wild and bloody world of experience enters in the form of King Charles, benighted on the hunt: "a madman—*steeped in blood*" (14). This wild, Dionysian figure is a foreshadowing of the Saint Bartholomew's Day massacre and the strife of the religious wars into which Gaston gradually moves. Also, the quarreling brothers Gaston encounters one night are in contrast to his ancestral brothers and their bond of familial devotion (and the affection of Ronsard and du Bellay or Montaigne and de la Boetie as well): "with a sudden flash of fierce words two young men burst from the doors of a roadside tavern. The brothers are quarrelling about the division, lately effected there, of their dead father's morsel of land. 'I shall hate you till death!' cries the younger, bounding away in the darkness; and two atheists part, to take opposite sides in the supposed strife of Catholic and Huguenot" (17–18). As the Saint Bartholomew's Day massacre, Pater notes, would come to be used to settle personal quarrels, so this private quarrel also finds its fulfillment in public strife. Through this public-private correspondence, the ancestral devotion of the Latour brothers is meant to be seen in nostalgic contrast to the looming conflict of the religious wars.

Paradoxically, as Gaston moves as a page into the cloistered life of the episcopal household at the cathedral of Chartres, the past is supplanted by the secular present—a present embodied in the "precocious worldliness" (36) of his fellow acolytes: "they had brought from their remote old homes all varieties of hereditary gifts, vices, distinctions, dark fates, mercy, cruelty, madness" (33). Like Pisa and Marius's friend Flavian, Chartres displays a "strange mixture of beauty and evil" (38), a discord characteristic of Ronsard's

poetry also, which Gaston shortly thereafter discovers. Prior
to his poetic awakening, the winter of 1567, the coldest
in a half-century, brought the siege of Chartres by the
Huguenots, imprisoning Gaston and his grandparents
among others within the city. In a curious detail obviously
included for thematic purposes, Pater narrates Gaston's
brush with death in a collapsing church "under a shower of
massy stones from the *coulevrines* or great cannon of the be-
siegers" (46), which is so similar to Marius's escape from the
falling rock of a landslide that one is tempted to apply to
Gaston's story the meaning of Marius's experience. Marius's
sense "of hatred against him, of the nearness of 'enemies' "
(*Marius*, 1: 166) shakes his Epicurean commitment to a life of
the senses; Gaston's commitment, on the other hand, had
been to a clerical calling which now in turn he abandons.
Pater additionally connects Gaston's brush with death with a
second powerful motive for change (he being an orphan): the
death of his grandmother in the midst of the siege. "That
broken link with life seemed to end some other things for
him" (*Gaston*, 47), that is, his vows and tonsure. There is also
here a connection with "The Child in the House," for just as
the empty house from which Florian rescues his trapped bird
"touched him like the face of one dead" (*Miscellaneous
Studies*, 196), so here Gaston gazes upon the cathedral of
Chartres "as he had gazed on the dead face" (*Gaston*, 47) of
his grandmother. But in contrast to Florian's homesickness,
Gaston has "no keen sense of personal loss" (47) when the
cathedral is despoiled by war because that childhood "link"
(10) between the church and the outer world—Saint Hubert's
filled with the visionary company in contrast to Chartres
emptied of its accumulated treasure—has now been
"broken."

At this crucial juncture in the preceding novel, Marius is
introduced to Cornelius and experiences a foretaste of the

resolution of his problem; Gaston, on the other hand, encounters a new profane religion. He visits Ronsard, having
already made the acquaintance of his odes. His court days
and his creative days over, Ronsard in middle age and failing
health was nonetheless not only lay superior of the Priory of
Croix-val but also the high priest of the worship of physical
beauty and liberty of heart and imagination. "Modernity"
begins with a submerged analogy between Gaston's relation
to his physical environment and his relation to literature.
After long confinement by siege, he is released into an open
countryside still charged with the peril of warfare; so, too,
the literature of the past—"chained to the bookshelf, like
something in a dead language, 'dead, and shut up in reliquaries of books' " (51)—is released by Ronsard's *Odes* and
*Amours* into a literary springtime charged with moral peril.
The landscape and the odes are related through the common
imagery of springtime—flowers, larks, fruit, heat, blossoms,
freshness—and both pose perils for the young and impres-
sionable Gaston. This movement of the chapter outward
from the "circle" of siege which shut up Gaston and the
others like "prisoners" (45) into the perilous, impassioned,
and troubling landscape is repeated in the visit to Ronsard.
First, Gaston crosses the "outer ring of blue up-lands" (58);
next, the poet appears within "the high espaliered garden-
wall, . . . visible through the open doors" (61). The open
doors of the church of Saint Hubert and of Ronsard's "enchanted castle" (61) promise escape (actual or illusory) from
the solipsism of the self "ringed round, . . . each mind keeping as a solitary prisoner its own dream of a world" (*Renaissance*, 235).

Often, in Pater's description of the development of his
characters, a literary discovery is suddenly the textual prelude to their maturer manhood: Winckelmann's sudden,
fervent awakening to the glory of antiquity through surrep-

titious reading of his master's Greek classics or Emerald Uthwart's and the English poet's leap of intellectual awakening. Sometimes this passion for an aesthetic, intellectual, or emotional ideal is effected by a single book: Apuleius's *Metamorphoses* with Marius or Duke Carl's accidental unearthing of Conrad Celtes's *Ars versificandi*. So too the eighteen-year-old Gaston, fresh from the cathedral school at Chartres, discovered for the first time the excitement of contemporary poetry in Ronsard's recent *Odes*. In his Postscript to *Appreciations*, Pater spoke of the periodic revitalization of classic forms by the romantic impulse, which in *Marius* he depicted as accomplished by the Frontonian revival and which in *Gaston* Ronsard effected for Virgil. Pater notes that Ronsard's *Odes* "took possession of Gaston with the ready intimacy of one's equal in age" (*Gaston*, 51). Since Ronsard published his *Odes* two years prior to Gaston's birth, the text has just that slight discrepancy in years as does Gaston's double, Charles; but unlike the antagonistic doppelgänger, Gaston enjoys a fraternal unity with the poems and hence a filial relation with Ronsard, the textual father. Just as in the essay on Michelangelo Pater had found that artist-poet to be "in possession of our inmost thoughts" (*Renaissance*, 95–96), so analogously Ronsard "seemed but to have spoken what was already in Gaston's own mind" (*Gaston*, 55). Looking up from his reading of Ronsard's unfinished manuscript, the *Franciade*, Gaston is suddenly himself read as a "legible document" by the poet who becomes "paternally anxious" for his furtherance (69).

Although Ronsard's poetry offers a renewal and freedom, it asks too steep a price by demanding that Gaston sever ties completely with his heritage of Deux-manoirs. In this, Ronsard's book of poetry is closest to Apuleius's Golden Book, for Gaston can no more be satisfied with Ronsard than Marius had been with Apuleius. Perhaps because he could not truly reconcile faith with art, Ronsard had failed to keep alive the fires of the fresh modernity of his youth, its romanticism, and so Gaston must push on. At Ronsard's recommendation, Gaston goes further south to the Gironde to visit Michel de Montaigne in his tower-library by the Dordogne. When about 1569 Gaston visited Montaigne, the *Essais* were unwritten, but Pater has Montaigne weave a cento of their contents in a nine-month discussion with his guest. As Ronsard had been the equivalent to Apuleius in *Marius*, so Montaigne the skeptic (as did Emerson, Pater overemphasizes Montaigne's skepticism) corresponds to Lucian. Lucian would have agreed with Montaigne that the "priceless pearl of truth" (93; *Marius*, 2: 168) does not inhere in any theory man can invent, for diversities of opinion are "themselves ultimate" (*Gaston*, 93). Indeed, Lucian suggests that those looking for some basic ground of truth are like temple guards searching among a host of secular cups, flagons, and diadems for a missing sacred vessel—neither shape nor material known, and unfortunately not inscribed with the name of its divine owner. And to the young Pater's insistence in "Coleridge's Writings" on the inevitable failure of all efforts to label and so identify that cup/dogma for all time, both Lucian and Montaigne would have subscribed: "Theology is a great house, scored all over with hieroglyphics by perished hands. When we decypher one of those hieroglyphics, we find in it the statement of a mistaken opinion; but knowledge has crept onward since the hand dropped from the wall; we no longer entertain the opinion, and we can trace the origin of the mistake."[7] Lucian still harbors a wistful longing after the impossible dream of discovering the cup, of deciphering the inscription, and finding the god: "And we too desire, not a fair one, but the fairest of all. Unless we find him, we shall think we have failed" (*Marius*, 2: 171).

7. Pater, "Coleridge's Writings," p. 129.

Montaigne's "undulant" philosophy, on the other hand, seems to rest content with the ultimacy of diversity. "But could one really care for truth, who never even seemed to find it?" Gaston asks himself concerning Montaigne. Perhaps, Gaston concedes (and Pater subtly puns on "ground" of being), "there was some deeper ground of thought in reserve; as if he were really moving, securely, over ground you did not see" (*Gaston*, 114–15).

In effect, Montaigne demonstrates as illusory or as merely provisional the possibilities implicit in Ronsard's verse for revitalization through a celebration of sensuous experience. Extending Ronsard theoretically, Montaigne is unable to suggest for the diverse world of thought and experience either an extrinsic or an intrinsic power of organization such as Gaston had known at Deux-manoirs; and the peril of Ronsard's poetry becomes explicit in Montaigne's tower: "How imperceptibly had darkness crept over them, effacing everything but the interior of the great circular chamber, its book-shelves and enigmatic mottoes and the tapestry on the wall,—Circe and her sorceries, in many parts,—to draw over the windows in winter. . . . Was Circe's castle here? If Circe could turn men into swine, could she also release them again?" (89–90). The darkening circular chamber, the windows of which are covered by the tapestry of Circe's castle on the wall, possesses a host of thematic filiations: with the encircled "solitary prisoner" of the dreaming mind, with Ronsard's "enchanted castle," with Marcus Aurelius's nearly "window-less" (*Marius*, 1: 216) audience chamber, with Apuleius's discourse in the darkness after the banquet. The moral diversity inherent in Ronsard's pursuit of the sensations of beauty and evil becomes in Montaigne's tower no longer a liberating landscape but leaves one in an imprisoning circle, "walled up suddenly, as if by malign trickery, in the open field" (*Gaston*, 100).

This ultimate failure of sensuous experience is a function of the growing self-consciousness of western culture:

> In the perplexed currents of modern thought, . . . the eternal problem of culture—balance, unity with one's self, consummate Greek modelling . . . [—]could no longer be solved . . . by perfection of bodily form, or any joyful union with the external world: the shadows had grown too long, the light too solemn, for that. . . . The chief factor in the thoughts of the modern mind concerning itself is the intricacy, the universality of natural law, even in the moral order. For us, necessity is not, as of old, a sort of mythological personage without us, with whom we can do warfare. It is rather a magic web woven through and through us, like that magnetic system of which modern science speaks, penetrating us with a network, subtler than our subtlest nerves, yet bearing in it the central forces of the world. Can art represent men and women in these bewildering toils so as to give the spirit at least an equivalent for the sense of freedom? . . . Natural laws we shall never modify, embarrass us as they may; but there is still something in the nobler or less noble attitude with which we watch their fatal combinations.
> [*Renaissance*, 228, 231]

If, since a web is a tapestry, we couple that "magic web woven through and through us" with the tapestry of Circe and, further, if modern man, caught in the "bewildering toils" (bewilder: AS *be* + *wild* + *deōr* to be covered with the wild beast; toils: MF *toile* net, fr. L *tela* web, fr. *texere* to weave) of natural laws, is connected with Circe's victims trapped in swine—if so, then Montaigne's tower has become the modern castle of Circe. What Pater is dramatizing in the circular tower-library is the emerging modern equivalent

(Montaigne's skepticism "does but commence the modern world" [*Plato*, 194]) to the antique and mythical form of entrapment. When the windows of Montaigne's darkening chamber ("the shadows had grown too long" for "joyful union with the external world") are covered in winter by the pictured castle of Circe ("a sort of mythological personage without us, with whom we can do warfare"), the tapestry portrays on the mythological level of an external battle of wills what by the covering of windows it also depicts on the symbolic level of an internal bondage. In effect, then, the double scene of Circe's castle on the wall of Montaigne's tower brilliantly depicts by complex equivalences the progress of western consciousness (particularly evident in the tower-library with "more books upon books than upon any other subject" [*Gaston*, 88]) from the Greeks to the Renaissance. To dramatize further the significance of this elaborate tableau, Pater has Gaston finish the chapter by playing at dice with Montaigne's young wife, enacting in play the role of mankind watching the "fatal combinations" of natural laws—and with Montaigne declining to join them because, as he explains, " 'play was not play enough, but too grave and serious a diversion' " (90)!

Although the transition from Montaigne's Circean tower to the bloodshed of 1572 constitutes a three-year jump in the life of Gaston, thematically it represents a mere shift from the game of dice to the "fatal combinations" of Saint Bartholomew's Eve. The circular tower of the modern Circe who thought diversities were ultimate is replaced by the city, which resembles "a prison or a *trap*" (126):

Delirium was in the air already charged with thunder, and laid hold on Gaston too. It was as if through some unsettlement in the atmospheric medium the objects around no longer acted upon the senses with the nor-

mal result. Looking back afterwards, this singularly
self-possessed person had to confess that under its influence he had lost for a while the exacter view of certain outlines, certain real differences and oppositions
of things in that hotly coloured world of Paris (like a
shaken tapestry about him) awaiting the Eve of Saint
Bartholomew. [124]

In the "shaken tapestry" of Paris the "quivering" carpet of La
Beauce reappears, yet in the unsettled atmosphere attending
the royal nuptials of Henry and Margaret the moral distinctions, the design or "outlines" manifest within the sanctuary
of Saint Hubert, are missing in the Louvre-castle-tower-city
of Circe's malign paradise: "Charles and his two brothers,
keeping the gates of a mimic paradise in the court of the
Louvre, while the fountains ran wine—were they already
thinking of a time when they would keep those gates, with
iron purpose, while the gutters ran blood?" (122). By enthrallment to sensual passion (or, since opposites meet, by
allegiance to some outworn dogma), the tapestry can lose its
central human design which opens from the narrow circle of
the present into that larger spirit of humanity and can become an "issueless circle" (*Imaginary Portraits*, 14) that traps
the soul like a bird (in the stone vaulting, the web between
the ribs, of Saint Vaast's in contrast to Saint Hubert's) or
can become what in the unpublished chapters Pater calls
an ever-revolving circle such as may be found, for example,
in mazes revolving perpetually into themselves as the one on
the cathedral floor at Chartres. Need one note that this reference to Chartres again contrasts it with Saint Hubert's?

In Gaston's marriage to the Huguenot Columbe, the
factional causes of Catholic and Protestant seek a private reconciliation, just as the two feuding houses in the portrait of
Denys had been reconciled by marriage. But Gaston's mar-

riage represents a potential for harmony that is almost imme-
diately frustrated by public events; and, by being painted
against the background of Gabrielle de Latour's story, his
tragedy has been sharpened. Gabrielle, watching at her window ten years for the return of her husband, had touched the
sleepy world of Deux-manoirs with "one of those grand passions, such as were needed to give life its true meaning and
effect" (Gaston, 21). In the Conclusion to The Renaissance,
Pater spoke of "great passions" and the "ecstasy and sorrow
of love" which give one a "quickened sense of life" (Renaissance, 238). Although such a "great" or "high" passion had
also forcibly moved Sebastian van Storck meditating on
Grotius's wife, Gabrielle's story approximates more closely
the Ceyx-Halcyon legend and the myth of Cupid and Psyche
as they formed themselves in Marius's imagination. This
constancy of Gaston's ancestor was a test of fidelity to an
ideal as strict as anything Psyche endured; and like Psyche's
bower of bliss, Gabrielle's chamber, expressive of that "great
passion of old," was for Gaston a "magic apartment"
(Gaston, 21–22). Much as Prior Saint-Jean, gazing longingly
from his window, had died upon the final permission to return to the valley of the monks, Gabrielle had "died of joy" at
that "wonderful moment" (20–21) of her husband's return.
Gabrielle's felicity of a hundred years before may have been
planned to be repeated in Gaston's life where "against all
expectation" (20) he too, perhaps, may have been reunited,
not with Columbe, his dead wife, but with his lost child.

As his grandmother's death, which counterpoints and
personalizes the mass deaths at Chartres, coincides with his
quitting the clerical vocation, so that "quiet double-holiday
morning" (128) on which Gaston's aged grandfather peace-
fully dies finalizes the irretrievable loss of harmony. The
doubleness of this holiday is only in one sense that of Sunday, 24 August, Feast of Saint Bartholomew; figuratively, it

is the contrast of deaths peaceful and violent, the fragmentation of wholeness into the antagonistic doppelgänger.
Elsewhere in Pater's fiction this slaughter of Saint Bartholomew's massacre and the death of Columbe is echoed in
Denys's death following a marriage, in the marriage-
martyrdom of the Gallic Christians in *Marius*, and most
closely in the obliteration of Duke Carl and his bride after the
death of the old grand duke of Rosenmold. One feels that
long, leisurely lives with scarcely perceptible endings are not
going to be numerous among Gaston's acquaintances, as the
Triumvirate's encounter with their bloody doubles foretells.
In the master trope of the tapestry, the fate of Gaston's young
friends is forecast: "Reappearing, from point to point, they
connected themselves with the great crimes, the great
tragedies of the time, as so many bright-coloured threads in
that sombre tapestry of human passion. . . . Threads to be cut
short, one by one, before his eyes, the three would cross and
recross, gaily, pathetically, in the tapestry of Gaston's years;
and, divided far asunder afterwards, seemed at this moment,
moving there before him in the confidential talk he could not
always share, inseparably linked together, like some complicated pictorial arabesque" (36, 49–50).

The fraternal double, no longer that of the brothers
Latour, has been reembodied now in the violently quarreling
brothers by the roadside tavern. And just as the antagonistic
brothers are an emblem on the private level of a public division, so a correspondence of private to public exists in the
fraternal opposition of the priestly Gaston to the royal
Charles IX. That the pathetic, blood-crazed Charles is
Gaston's opposing doppelgänger on the national level is evident from a number of analogues. Charles was born in 1550,
Gaston in 1552; thus, both are of an age (the slight discrepancy in years is suggested by the myth of the Dioscuri and
recurs in Pater's other pairings). Both undergo a ritual; as

Gaston is made a clerk in orders, "far away in Paris the young King Charles the Ninth, in his fourteenth year, has been just declared of age" (5). The reference at this point to the parallel *rites de passage* specifically stresses the association between royal and priestly careers. Most significantly, Charles, soaked in blood from his hunting expedition, stops at Deux-manoirs and sleeps for some hours in the love chamber of Gabrielle de Latour, the favorite haunt of Gaston. Charles's presence there suggests a reanimation of Gabrielle's antagonistic doppelgänger within Gaston's marriage-to-be—her sorrow for the absent mate will now become that of Gaston.

As a madman hunter, an effeminate winter Dionysus, bloody Charles (animal blood, not yet that of humans) significantly foreshadows the massacre of Saint Bartholomew's Eve and Gaston's guilt in it; for, paradoxically, the "madness" and "delirium" (116, 124, 127) of Paris on Saint Bartholomew's Eve belong as much to the hunted (Gaston-Columbe) as to the hunter (Charles, who literally had come to Deux-manoirs as a hunter):

> In the conception of Dionysus . . . a certain transference, or substitution, must be made—much of the horror and sorrow . . . of the whole tragic situation, must be transferred to him, if we wish to realise in the older, profounder, and more complete sense of his nature, that mystical being of Greek tradition to whom all these experiences—his madness, the chase, his imprisonment and death, his peace again—really belong. . . . Dionysus *Omophagus*—the eater of raw flesh, must be added to the golden image of Dionysus *Meilichius*—the honey-sweet, if . . . we are to catch, in its fulness, that deep undercurrent of horror which runs below, all through this masque of spring, and

realise the spectacle of that wild chase, in which
Dionysus is ultimately both the hunter and the spoil.
[*Greek Studies*, 78–79]

Madness, chase, imprisonment, death—these also describe
Paris and the massacre of 1572. And like Denys with "his
contrast, his dark or antipathetic side, . . . a double creature,
of two natures, difficult or impossible to harmonise" (*Imaginary Portraits*, 66), Gaston now has become both hunter and
hunted. By his predisposition to regard his own interfaith
marriage as a "mere mistake" or "unmeaning accident"
(*Gaston*, 126), Gaston is linked morally both to the "illicit and
inauspicious" (121) public nuptials of Protestant Prince
Henry and Catholic Margaret and to the ensuing, nearly accidental, marriage slaughter on Saint Bartholomew's Eve:
"not the cruelty only but the obscurity, the accidental
character, yet, alas! also the treachery, of the public event
seemed to identify themselves tragically with his own personal action, . . . had made him so far an accomplice in their
unfriendly action that he felt certainly not quite guiltless,
thinking of his own irresponsible, self-centered, passage
along the ways, through the weeks that had ended in the
public crime and his own private sorrow" (129), leaving with
him the sense "for the rest of his days of something like remorse" (120). Columbe's belief that she has been treacher-
ously deserted doubtless echoes Aliette's death in Pater's
1886 critical portrait, "Feuillet's '*La Morte*.' " There the husband,
Bernard, exclaims: "She died believing me guilty! . . . And
she will never, never know that it was not so; that I am innocent" (*Appreciations*, 238). Bernard's grief brings him to his
deathbed on which he is converted from unbelief to the religion of his wife—a pattern possibly to be repeated in
Gaston's turn to the Huguenot belief of Columbe.

Pater allows fourteen years to elapse after the 1572 massacre before resuming the thread of his narrative in the next and, as the novel now stands, final chapter. If from Montaigne the skeptic Gaston learned of the relativity of values and the diversity of opinions, afterward from Giordano Bruno, who came to Paris in 1579 and is lecturing at the Sorbonne in 1586, he is initiated into an idealism that preached the spiritual unity of creation. But just as Ronsard's enthrallment to physical sensation turns out to have much in common with the intellectual skepticism of Montaigne, so Montaigne's skepticism also has much in common with Bruno's religious mysticism. Good and evil are still perilously allied: "If God the Spirit had made, nay! was, all things indifferently, then, matter and spirit, the spirit and the flesh, heaven and earth, freedom and necessity, the first and the last, good and evil, would be superficial rather than substantial differences" (*Gaston*, 143–44). But juxtaposed with the massacre in which Gaston suffers the personal loss of his wife and child (not to mention the more general loss of life), Bruno's refusal to recognize the reality of evil is powerfully condemned. In this respect, Bruno's refusal to see evil is much like Marcus Aurelius's moral blindness, for just as Aurelius sponsored the "Manly Amusement" of the amphitheater and the martyrdom of the Gallic Christians, so Bruno is—retrospectively—the intellectual sponsor of the massacre of Saint Bartholomew's Eve. Although the pluralism of Montaigne's diverse entities which negate any Absolute Spirit is supplanted by the monism of Bruno's Spirit who negates finite reality, the common *practical* result (always the touchstone for Pater) of their theoretical indifference or inclusiveness is the immorality of Gaston's Paris.

In the unpublished chapters, Queen Margaret of Navarre—Margot of the *Memoirs*—is explicitly presented as a Renaissance Circe whose palace is the Louvre and whose enchanted island is Paris. In his chronicles, Brantôme, a dis-

ciple of Montaigne's and Bruno's seeming license to accord
aesthetic values pride of place over moral values, eloquently
portrays Margot as the femme fatale of her age. Not just the
Circe on Montaigne's wall but the idolized ladies of Ronsard's verse had prefigured Brantôme's sorceress: the pagan
goddess Minerva took the place of Our Lady in Ronsard's
apartment, "bringing the odd, enigmatic physiognomy,
preferred by the art of that day, within the sphere of religious
devotion" (64); and on the walls of Ronsard's study his ladies
"might have been sisters, those many successive loves, or
one and the same lady over and over again" (64). Circe,
Minerva, Ronsard's loves: Margot's multiplicity is not unlike
that of Mona Lisa, and her face seems to haunt the art of her
age, not as the priceless pearl of truth as her name would
suggest (65) but as the visible form of an unseen force of cruel
love. After the fashion of Circe's Ulysses, Gaston is
enthralled by the spectacle of Margot's exotic religion of car-
nal beauty. Our Lady of Chartres of his consecrated youth
has become the temptress of the Louvre, a modulation from
innocence to corruption reminiscent of Demeter's daughters
as Pater had described them in *Greek Studies*. As amanuensis,
Gaston serves Margot much as Marius had served Marcus
Aurelius, although Aurelius's lofty spirituality lay at the opposite extreme from Margot's sensual disavowal of the
spiritual realm. This narcissism is initially evident to Gaston
in the house of Margot's lover, Jasmin, in which a decorative
pseudoclassicism fails to capture the true classical harmony
of sense and spirit (that problem of balance no longer to be
solved by any mere "perfection of bodily form"). A volume
of the *Meditations* of Marcus Aurelius causes Gaston to sense
that in Jasmin's empty house not only is the human form
absent (as it was in Circe's swine) but its spirit also has been
destroyed by being enthralled to sensuality. (Ironically, Aurelius had been presented in *Marius* as a despiser of the

body, his empty palace revealing a moral isolation as disastrous in its way as the elaborate but lifeless "aestheticism" of Jasmin's mannered dwelling.) Only in the painted glass of Jean Cousin, who rejuvenates the old Gothic under the influence of the Italian style, and in the work of the modern Italian masters themselves, such as da Vinci, does Gaston find a power capable of "linking paternally, filially, age to age."[8] Their portraiture reconstitutes the living human form absent among the elaborately balanced harmonies of Jasmin's empty house.

Montaigne's tapestry of the flux has no central design; diversity is ultimate. Bruno's tapestry has centers everywhere; none is preeminent. But that paternal-filial linking of age to age so evident in the ritual at Saint Hubert's and in the emphatically historical existence of Deux-manoirs from the Middle Ages to the Revolution suggests there can be an ongoing human center perpetually reconstituted from age to age. Yet, if one interprets the idea of family in Pater's work to include all who feel ties of a spousal, parental, or fraternal nature, one notices that his writings are positively haunted by the theme of the divided family, of severed ties; and, indeed, a corresponding quest for reunion constitutes the central plot suspense (though *suspense* is too strong a term) for *Gaston de Latour* as a whole. Although Columbe has definitely died (130), Pater evidently intended Gaston's search for his lost child to culminate in a reunion at his death. Many of Pater's heroes, questing after that reunion which symbolizes the reintegration of sense and spirit, find themselves reliving ritual or mythic patterns, finally sacrificing their very lives to their foreordained roles. Even mythic instances of spousal or paternal-maternal reunion, as in the tale of Cupid and Psyche or the story of Demeter and Persephone, involve a descent into the underworld; more emphatically

8. d'Hangest, *Pater*, 2: 365 n. 19.

among mortals, this reunion, as Duke Carl's return to Gretchen, is sealed by death.

Seemingly, only by sacrificing the physical continuity of the Latour family in the ritual at Saint Hubert's is Gaston able to reconstitute the ideal human image within the tapestry. Analogously, at the Christmas Mass in *Marius*, the past is reanimated only by the crucified Christ, who "seemed to have absorbed, like some rich tincture in his garment, all that was deep-felt and impassioned in the experiences of the past" (*Marius*, 1: 134). The deeply dyed vesture of Christ and the "many-coloured carpet" of La Beauce appear also in the "strange dyes, strange colours" of the flux as caught for a few moments in those "strange webs" for which Mona Lisa traffics, webs produced, she knows, by "that strange perpetual weaving and unweaving of ourselves" (*Renaissance*, 237, 125, 236). "Strange," because the design in the web is at once new and wonderful but, also, latent with ."the fatality which seems to haunt any signal beauty" (*Marius*, 1: 93). All of these images center in the master symbol of the blood on the arena's sand in which the human form, that "design in a web," is redeemed from death by its reenactment in the present. As Pater notes in *Plato* (substituting cultural history for Wordsworth's clouds of glory): "we come into the world, each one of us, 'not in nakedness,' but . . . clothed . . . in a vesture of the past, nay, fatally shrouded, it might seem, in those laws or tricks of heredity which we mistake for our volitions" (*Plato*, 72). And one of those small acts of devotion that Gaston recollects when he hears of Montaigne's seemingly pious end—one of those concessions to "a certain great possibility, which might lie among the conditions of so complex a world" (*Gaston*, 113), that takes Montaigne one step beyond the ultimacy of diversity—is his wrapping himself in "an old mantle that had belonged to his father. Retained, . . . in spite of its inconvenience, 'because it seemed to envelope

me in him,' it was the symbol of a hundred natural, perhaps
somewhat material, pieties. Parentage, kinship, relationship
through earth,—the touch of that was everywhere like a
caress to him" (107).

Owing to Pater's concept of identity as expressive of the
composite experience of history—the self ceaselessly tra-
versed by codes of meaning like threads through a tapestry—any given moment in time represents a "retrac-
ing" (*Marius*, 1: 134) or "reminiscence" (*Renaissance*, 194;
*Plato*, 67) of previously existing moments. Thus Gaston,
lodged in Abelard's quarter, "all but repeats Abelard's typical *experience*" (*Gaston*, 124) since, like Abelard and Héloïse,
Gaston and Columbe are tragically divided. Repetition or
"Imitation:—it enters into the very fastnesses of character;
and we, our souls, ourselves, are for ever imitating what we
see and hear, the forms, the sounds which haunt our
memories, our imagination. We imitate not only if we play a
part on the stage but when we sit as spectators, while our
thoughts follow the acting of another, when we read Homer
and put ourselves, lightly, fluently, into the place of those he
describes" (*Plato*, 272). One might note the numerous references to stage plays in *Gaston* as elaborating this motif of the
reenactment of the past within the present, but the most pervasive instance of "imitation" in Gaston's experience and the
one which best illuminates Pater's projected design for his
unfinished romance is the Homeric account of Ulysses' jour-
ney home from Troy to Ithaca. Possibly Charles Lamb's *Ad-
ventures of Ulysses*, which unlike typical nineteenth-century
translations presented realistic characters who also signified
"external force or internal temptations,"[9] encouraged Pater
to adapt Homer's epic for his own symbolic ends.

Since for Pater both the self and its repetitions are mul-

9. From Lamb's preface, cited and discussed in W. B. Stanford, *The Ulysses Theme* (Oxford: B. Blackwell, 1954), pp. 186–87.

tiform, *Gaston*'s parallels with *The Odyssey* move on several
historical planes simultaneously and are modified by a large
number of non-Homeric correspondences from literature and
history. If Queen Margot is Circe and Gaston Ulysses, Gabrielle de Latour, who lived a century before, plays the part of
(a) Penelope: "Here certainly she had watched, at these windows, during ten whole years, for the return of her beloved
husband from a disastrous battle in the East, till against all
expectation she beheld him crossing the court at last"
(*Gaston*, 20). Of course, Gabrielle is not only Penelope—no
one is merely *one*—and the fact that she "died of joy" upon
her husband's return owes less to Homer than to Pliny's
"Roman lady who died for joy to see her son return alive
from the rout at Cannae" (to quote—appropriately, consid-
ering Gaston's own experience—Montaigne's "Of Sorrow").[10] Given such an interweaving of sources, one might
worry about "overreading" Homeric echoes were it not that
the episode of Gabrielle connects itself forcefully with
another event so that, combined, they present an inescapable
Odyssean parallel. At Chartres, Gaston beholds "a strange
maritime personage, stout and square, returned, contrary to
all expectation, after ten years' captivity among the savages
of Florida" (44), whose matted hair and outlandish hands
and face suggest tenure as one of Circe's swine. Not only was
Ulysses a "maritime personage," but the echo of "against all
expectation" in "contrary to all expectation" leaps the gap of
a century to fuse Gabrielle's belated warrior with Gaston's
captured sailor into a single Homeric archetype. Finally, the
decade common to both episodes corresponds precisely to
the interval Ulysses wandered after the fall of Troy.

This Homeric correspondence would have provided a
major level of meaning for the completed text with Gaston's
return to Deux-manoirs. Excluded, of course, would be a

10. Montaigne, *Essais*, 1: ii.

final Homeric-style shoot-out and triumphant reunion; for in Pater's projected version of the tale, Penelope-Columbe (or her equivalent, the missing child) symbolizes Gaston's lost wholeness. As both the seeker and the one sought, she is the goal of Gaston's quest to overcome his divided and conflicting self, that inner antagonism which is externalized in the general warfare of the age. From this angle, Penelope's deferred choice of a suitor in Ulysses' absence is akin to Montaigne's "suspended judgment" or to Lucian's skeptical refusal to accept any particular scheme as possessing final truth. Like Lucian, she too longs not for a fair one, "but the fairest of all." Additionally, that famous Web of Penelope, "never ending, still beginning," would lead inevitably back to the master trope of the tapestry, Penelope (like the web-trafficking Mona Lisa) being an embodiment of "that eternal process of nature, . . . the 'Living Garment,' whereby God is seen of us, ever in weaving at the 'Loom of Time' " (Marius, 1: 129). Clearly Gaston-as-Ulysses can never hope to find Columbe-as-Penelope within the plot of the novel because she herself is the eternal process both of weaving and of all things woven, including that ultimate symbol of the web, the text (L texere to weave) itself. The real drama of Gaston's quest for Columbe has shifted from the plot to the next frame out; and on this level the text dramatizes the act of artistic creation. Gaston, now the collective mind of his age, has become a textuality in search of an author.

Clearly Homer's tale came too close to the conventional historical romance and had to be reconstituted by Pater in such a way that Ulysses' triumphant reunion with Penelope would dramatize the immediate act of its own recomposition. The Odyssey reflected the unself-conscious mind of the Greek who supposed man's will to be limited by "a sort of mythological personage without us, with whom we can do warfare," but the growing self-consciousness of western culture will not permit an art built upon such assumptions: "That naïve, rough sense of freedom, which supposes man's will to be limited, if at all, only by a will stronger than his, he can never have again. The attempt to represent it in art would have so little verisimilitude that it would be flat and uninteresting" (*Renaissance*, 231). Pater rejects low-mimetic "formal realism" because it fails to recognize the limits of documentary or naturalistic description. To treat the categories of time, space, matter, and identity as if they were static falsifies the actual character of experience, which is a continuous, changing process grasped only in terms of the subjective perceptions of the individual. Only by substituting autobiographical processes and problems of perception for the external actions of conventional fiction can an elusive outer reality be replaced by a self-sustaining imaginative reality. As Pater writes: "all true knowledge will be like the knowledge of a person, of living persons, and truth, . . . to the last, something to *look* at," adding that "human persons and their acts" are visible representations "of the eternal qualities of 'the eternal' " (*Plato*, 146, 268). In conventional fiction there is no consciousness opening itself to the reader, no mental or personal reality which, reembodied by the innermost self of the reader, can summon back into life the author's feelings and ideas. Authors who produce realistic novels share Hermotimus's quixotic aspiration to find Lucian's inscribed cup, to find and fix an objective truth within the flux. And yet Hermotimus's hope is ironically undercut as he sits among those "sepulchral inscriptions" (*Marius*, 2: 170) on the Appian Way. Like theological truths among funereal "hieroglyphics" or originality in "reliquaries of books," the design isolated from the vitality of the web is merely a lifeless textual husk—epitaph, hieroglyphic, or reliquary. What the visionary text does, however, is perpetually return the design to the life of the web, allowing it to

escape final formulation as it slips back into that larger flow
of personality through time from which it originally came.
Although such a text cannot catch external reality in its net of
words, as the realistic novel purports to do, it can approach
the structure of reality asymptotically through an ongoing
dialectic between consciousnesses. Within the scope of the
plot, Gaston can never adequately recapture his lost wholeness; that wholeness can be reestablished only through the
interplay of his story with the next frame out—the authorial
level of inscription.

Pater's notion of the textual Other in which the author
seeks "deliverance from mortality" (*Marius*, 1: 97) is brilliantly worked out in terms of the Homeric theme of Telemachus and Ulysses, each in search of the other. Pater, as
author and orphaned son longing for a father, and his
specular double within the text, Gaston, as the father questing for his son, jointly constitute that lost paternal-filial
wholeness which only the dialectic between inner and outer
levels of self and Other can restore. In the preexisting texts
that he reweaves imaginatively from the culture of the sixteenth century, Pater finds his father. But just as Telemachus
and Ulysses are absorbed into and idealized by the figure of
Penelope and her eternal weaving and unweaving, so Pater
begets, simultaneously with the recovery of his own father,
a nineteenth-century textual son which in its (his) turn will
quest as a father for a vitalizing reunion with some future
son. Not only is "the old over-written pavement" at the great
open door of Saint Hubert's literally a record of fathers and
sons, but as a palimpsestic web it symbolizes the eternal
*textual* creation of the filial present by the paternal past and
the corresponding re-creation of the now filial past by the
paternal present. The bloody Charles IX, whose last words
"had asserted his satisfaction in leaving no male child to
wear his crown" (*Gaston*, 136), represents a failure to recog-

nize this centrality of the paternal-filial design within the web of history, and his sentiment contrasts sharply with, for example, the Latours' sense of family life being "like a second sacred history" (4) or that saving instinct which enveloped Montaigne in the vesture of his paternal mantle. Circe's prison of low-mimetic formal realism, of that "false impression of permanence or fixity in things," can be escaped not by discovering "some scheme of truth . . . in some penetrative mind" outside one's own perceptions but rather by locating truth in the subjectivities of seeing itself, which by the act of writing become objectified, like the returned Ulysses, as "something to *look* at." What would not Pater as a child have given to have heard with Telemachus the words: "I am that father whom your boyhood lacked and suffered pain for lack of. I am he."[11] Pater the adult both heard and himself uttered these words every time he wrote.

11. *The Odyssey* (book 16), trans. Robert Fitzgerald (Garden City, N.Y.: Doubleday, 1963), p. 295. Just before his mystical encounter at the Sabine inn with "the *Father of Men*" (*Marius*, 2: 68), Marius has "a dream, in which, as once before, he overheard those he loved best pronouncing his name very pleasantly, as they passed through the rich light and shadow of a summer morning, along the pavement of a city—Ah! fairer far than Rome!" (2: 63). If this is understood autobiographically, it suggests the absent father naming Pater his son as *pater*, a father.

CHAPTER FIVE

# Beauty and Evil

*Gaston*, like *Marius*, was designed to be another instance of
Pater's recovery of his father and another vindication of the
impotent Oxford don's paternal potency. What went wrong?
Why did he fail to complete his novel? To begin with the
textual father: if Gaston is an autobiographically transposed
version of Pater himself, a volume of verse analogous to that
of Ronsard's *Odes* should have been discovered by Pater in
his own eighteenth year. Gosse affirms that Pater at nineteen
was deeply affected by his reading of Ruskin's *Modern Painters;* then, too, Morris's 1858 volume of verse conveys something of the freshness and surprise of the life of the senses
that Ronsard's poetry exerted on Gaston.[1] But the volume
that seems most likely to have been personally for Pater
a parallel influence was, appropriately, by a French poet.
In 1857, in Pater's eighteenth year, Baudelaire published
*Les fleurs du mal.* Clearly Baudelaire is for Pater what Ronsard is for Gaston, for Pater describes Ronsard's *Odes* as
"sweet, but with something of the sickliness of all spring
flowers since the days of Proserpine"; and in concluding
his chapter, Pater writes that Gaston's new worship of
beauty was a profane religion in which "there were 'flowers of evil,' among the rest" (*Gaston,* 51, 71). Pater, then, fresh
from his own cathedral school of Canterbury, discovered
in Baudelaire what Gaston had found in Ronsard, and
he ever after remained occupied, like Gaston, with the

1. Gosse, *Kit-Kats,* p. 247; Pater, "Poems by William Morris," pp. 300–12.

137

philosophical question concerning "the entanglement of
beauty with evil—to what extent one might succeed in disentangling them or, failing that, how far one may warm and
water the dubious, double root, watch for its flower, or retain
the hope, or the memory, or the mere tokens of it in one's
keeping."[2]

If *Marius* had been designed to demonstrate to those
young men of 1873, so easily misled by the Conclusion to *The
Renaissance*, that beauty has an ethical function which cannot
be disavowed, *Gaston*, as the second work of the projected
trilogy, equally concerned itself with the "disentangling" of
that "dubious, double root" of beauty and evil. But by the
late 1880s those young men—Wilde, Symons, and others—
were increasingly preoccupied with the celebration of ec-
static moments isolated within the flux of sensations. In
pursuing the ecstasy of the gemlike flame, Pater's sons were
apostate or, rather, too faithful to the latent textual paternity
of Baudelaire—as the publication in 1890 of Wilde's *Picture of
Dorian Gray* evinced.[3] Dorian, a youthful figure of age-old

2. Quoted in d'Hangest, *Pater*, 2: 364 n. 15. In the first third of the 1877
"Giorgione" essay, Pater's discussion of form and matter and of the relation
of music to painting is clearly indebted to Baudelaire's *L'art romantique*.
Further, three significant references to Baudelaire the previous year in
"Romanticism" establish Pater's knowledge not only of *L'art romantique* but,
by identifying Baudelaire as a lover of animals, of *Les fleurs du mal* also, with
its cats, swan, and albatross. Arthur Symons persuasively compares a passage from the Morris essay (reprinted as "Aesthetic Poetry") with lines from
Baudelaire on "the effects of Haschisch" and infers that Pater's study "was
evidently written under the influence of Baudelaire, whose prose, as he
himself told me, he admired intensely." Symons, *A Study of Walter Pater*
(London: Sawyer, 1932), pp. 69–70; see also *Renaissance*, ed. Symons, p. xx.
If Pater had not actually read *Les fleurs du mal* as early as 1857, one must
nevertheless admit that in writing *Gaston* he autobiographically implied it;
thus, a fictional work makes an indirect autobiographical statement which
may be, in its turn, a fiction—yet true to life.

3. d'Hangest calls attention to Pater's effort in *Gaston* to answer Wilde's
misguided discipleship, noting that Pater had originally intended Wilde's
"Live up to your blue china" to serve as an epigraph for chapter 8. *Pater*, 2:
363 n. 9.

experience, was in essence a remastering of Pater's Mona
Lisa image in terms of the supposedly hedonistic Conclusion. In the opening words of his work, Wilde had saluted
Pater's image of Mr. Rose, the decadent: "The studio was
filled with the rich odour of roses."[4] But what especially
must have perturbed Pater was the discovery that his own
text had been echoed verbally in the novel, Wilde's chapter 11
in particular being a reweaving, in typical Paterian fashion,
of key passages from the Conclusion. After 1890 a noticeable
estrangement occurred between Pater and Wilde (as well as
between Pater and Symons); in his review of Dorian Gray,
Pater spoke rather sharply of the heroes' (meaning the
book's) loss of "the moral sense, . . . the sense of sin and
righteousness."[5]

Yet how could righteousness and beauty exist unentan-
gled with the fallenness of sensuous experience? In his
schoolboy poem "Watchman, what of the night?" the young
Pater had desired to hear "the high Archangel's call" which
would summon him from the sensuous flux of space and
time to the "Unchanged Eternity" of Christ. Later, discus-
sing a similar haven of art which would perpetuate the
fleeting moments of life, Pater wrote in a passage deleted
after its first appearance in "The School of Giorgione":
"Who, in some such perfect moment, when the harmony of
things inward and outward beat itself out so truly, and with
a sense of receptivity, as if . . . some messenger from the real
soul of things must be on his way to one, has not felt the

4. As early as 1876 in Mallock's New Republic (first serialized in Belgravia
from June to December 1876), Wilde is connected with Pater. There Mr. Rose
reads to the company a parody of one of Wilde's recently published sonnets,
"written by a boy of eighteen—a youth of extraordinary promise, I think,
whose education I may myself claim to have had some share in directing."
W. H. Mallock, The New Republic (London: Chatto and Windus, 1877), book
4, chapter 1.

5. Pater, "A Novel by Mr. Oscar Wilde," Sketches and Reviews (New
York: Boni and Liveright, 1919), p. 132.

desire to perpetuate all that, just so . . . —a desire how bewildering with the question whether there be indeed any
place wherein these desirable moments take permanent refuge. Well! in the school of Giorgione you drink water, perfume, music, lie in receptive humour thus for ever, and the
satisfying moment is assured."[6] Yet the problem is that the
Archangel who comes as "messenger" (angel: Gk. *angelos*
messenger) from the place of "refuge" is ultimately an ambiguous envoy, beneficent and threatening, for the decentered origin or ground of reality can be focused only by
a perpetual passage of untranslatable moments across the
abyss of nonbeing. Only within the structure of art itself can
the ideal moment in any sense be "assured."

To understand the tension between the disintegrating
effect of the world of the flux, threateningly naturalistic and
pagan, and that elusive wholeness glimpsed within the aesthetic object, one must go back to one of Pater's earliest
portraits, that of J. J. Winckelmann. Pater's temperamental
affinity with Winckelmann, the wanderer seeking a spiritual
home whose life's work was so devastatingly cut short, was
perhaps stronger than with any other figure in *The Renaissance*, even that of Leonardo. Some eight or nine years after
"Watchman," in describing Winckelmann's "romantic, fervent friendships with young men," Pater writes that
Winckelmann "has known, he says, many young men more
beautiful than Guido's archangel. These friendships, bringing him into contact with the pride of human form, and
staining the thoughts with its bloom, perfected his reconciliation to the spirit of Greek sculpture" (*Renaissance*, 191). Here
the epiphany of the archangel is, quite explicitly, envisioned
as the sexual lover whose presence "stains" the innocence of
the mind with its "bloom." This ambiguous lover reappears
a few pages later, now unambiguously in the guise of a mur-

6. Pater, "The School of Giorgione," *Fortnightly Review* 22 (1877): 536.

derer. Winckelmann had set out from Rome to visit his native Germany, but "as he left Rome, a strange, inverted
home-sickness, a strange reluctance to leave it at all, came
over him"; he departs from Vienna "intending to hasten
back to Rome, and at Trieste a delay of a few days occurred.
With characteristic openness, Winckelmann had confided
his plans to a fellow-traveller, a man named Arcangeli, and
had shown him the gold medals received at Vienna. Arcangeli's avarice was aroused. One morning he entered
Winckelmann's room, under pretence of taking leave.
Winckelmann was then writing 'memoranda for the future
editor of the *History of Art*,' still seeking the perfection of his
great work. Arcangeli begged to see the medals once more.
As Winckelmann stooped down to take them from the chest,
a cord was thrown round his neck" (195–96). And so died
Winckelmann, not the first to discover that you can't go
home again. Pater's evenness of tone here bespeaks an almost rigid suppression of the ironic significance of the assas-
sin's name and the latently homosexual circumstances under
which the murder occurred. Here the "Archangel's call" does
not draw Winckelmann to the "truth sublime" of the
"Watchman" but leaves him grotesquely strangled between
his two homelands, Germany and Italy.

What becomes of Pater's youthful dread of annihilation,
his adolescent fear that "the high Archangel's call" may not,
after all, be heard, is his later unconscious sense that the
call of the Archangel, now "Mr Archangels," might be perhaps a murderous encounter by a treacherous lover. In the
penumbra of apocryphal stories surrounding Pater's life in
Thomas Wright's two volume *Life* (1907), the curious figure of
Mr. Archangels crops up once more in just this ambivalent
way. Wright's second volume is practically a wholesale
transcript of the pathological fantasies of a south London
eccentric in which Pater is characterized as a fawning

sycophant; and standing as it does at the biographical head-waters, Wright's travesty is possibly more sinister than Ian Fletcher's barbed summary of it as "one of the (unintentionally) comic masterpieces of our literature" might suggest. In this second volume, Wright describes Pater's presence at the house of the eccentric Richard Jackson when near midnight the housekeeper announced "that there was a tremendous fellow—a complete stranger—standing on the step with something wrapped in a black cloth, who—and she confided to them that she did not like either his appearance or his manner—declared that he would see nobody but Mr. Jackson. Noticing his friend hesitate, Pater said, 'Go at once. It might be an archangel sent to you direct from Heaven.'" At the door was a burly laborer bringing Jackson a linnet in a cage "'because, sir, you have been so kind to me and my poor mother.'" Pater, "half in tears," remarked "in a husky voice, 'I told you it might be an archangel sent direct from Heaven; and so it is.'" In an additional anecdote, Wright describes how, as Pater looked on, this fellow, "who from the day of the linnet incident was known as 'The Archangel,'" flattened with his "gigantic fist" a man who had mocked Jackson in his cassock.[7] Whatever actually may have been the details of this outrageous "reminiscence"—probably Jackson's fantasizing was prompted by some initial *donnée* (though the flattened man surely did not get up and, as alleged, kiss the hem of Jackson's gown)—the manifestation of an ambiguous force malign and protective precisely corresponds to Pater's sense of the lover who slays. Will the archangel throw a rope around one's neck or, as the "Watchman" says of Christ, reveal that "Thou lovest and art just"?

This angel-lover, a kind of flowering from the "dubious, double root" of beauty and evil, appears either as "divine

7. Wright, *Pater*, 2: 46–47.

companion," betokening an ideal moment of unity when the self is present to itself in all of its multiplicity, or as "antagonist," typifying a negative state of dividedness in which that wholeness is absent. In Marius's vision at the inn in the Sabine hills the complementarity of this relationship is stressed; Marius senses the presence of a "divine companion" who "figured no longer as but an occasional wayfarer beside him; but rather as the unfailing 'assistant,' without whose inspiration and concurrence he could not breathe or see, instrumenting his bodily senses, rounding, supporting his imperfect thoughts. . . . How he had longed, sometimes, that there were indeed one to whose boundless power of memory he could commit his own most fortunate moments, . . . one strong to retain them even though he forgot, in whose more vigorous consciousness they might subsist for ever" (*Marius*, 2: 70–71). But in his recollection of this experience Marius afterward remembers another presence in *combat* with him (presumably this companion, "without whose inspiration [*in-* in + *spirare* to breathe] and concurrence he could not breathe," now has Mr. Archangels's rope around his ontological neck): "Through the train of my thoughts, one against another, it was as if I became aware of the dominant power of another person in controversy, wrestling with me. I seem to be come round to the point at which I left off then. The antagonist has closed with me again" (2: 184). Earlier, this grappling opponent had been foreshadowed by the picture of the wrestling angel in Florian's books: "He pored over the pictures in religious books, and knew by heart the exact mode in which the wrestling angel grasped Jacob. . . . His way of conceiving religion came then to be . . . a sacred ideal, a transcendent version or representation, under intenser and more expressive light and shade, of human life . . . —a mirror, towards which men might turn away their eyes from vanity and dullness, and see themselves therein as angels" (*Miscellaneous Studies*, 193–94). The logic of the passage says that the pictured angel wrestling in discord with Jacob is also, as an episode of sacred history, a mirror version of Jacob's concordant self.

In this encounter with the Other, the quotidian self of "vanity and dullness" is radically transformed, to be replaced by that transcendent self "assured" by art. Thus, although his thigh was thrown out of joint by the stranger, Jacob also was renamed (interestingly, Pater too was injured in a scuffle which left him as an adult with impaired gait). Likewise, at the precise moment when the archangel summoned Winckelmann, he was writing "'memoranda for the future editor of the *History of Art*,' still seeking the perfection of his great work." It was to be a perfection brought to fruition by someone else, but not necessarily an editor of the *History*. Because of Winckelmann's murder, the nineteen-year-old Goethe (the same age as the Pater who had composed "Watchman") is thwarted in his chance for "one of those famous friendships, the very tradition of which becomes a stimulus to culture, and exercises an imperishable influence." Nevertheless, remarks Pater, "as it was, Winckelmann became to him something like what Virgil was to Dante" (*Renaissance*, 197). Winckelmann, whose friendships stained his thoughts, finds also that they have "perfected his reconciliation to the spirit of Greek sculpture"; and it is this renamed or "transcendent version" of Winckelmann embodied in the *History* which becomes a Virgilian guide—the divine or angelic assistant—to Goethe. Here present is an ongoing dialectic between the antique sculpture that fosters Winckelmann's maturing talent and a reciprocal re-creation of antiquity through Winckelmann's surrendering or relinquishing himself to the *History*. This text then fosters in Goethe another writer who in his turn will surrender himself to a textual identity—and so on until in 1873 cultural history produces *Studies in the History of the Renaissance.*

But what of those whose thoughts *The Renaissance* had not merely fostered but actually had stained? After Lord Henry's and Dorian's "new hedonism," Pater's fear of misleading his disciples with Baudelairean flowers of evil had intensified. Unable for this reason to finish *Gaston,* he instead was driven to explain himself in two shorter portraits, "Emerald Uthwart" and "Apollo in Picardy." The heroes of each are victims of society's tendency to deny or fear the life of the senses. In the first portrait the hero, as his name implies, is a gemlike figure of youth thwarted, the victim of a value system unwilling to allow a decentered authority; the hero of the second, likewise a victim of perverse cultural assumptions, mistakenly attempts to capture in abstract formulas the fundamental nature of reality and is unable to complete his life's work. The flux cannot be disavowed, nor the senses disowned.

In "Emerald Uthwart" Pater returned toward the end of his career in 1892 to those formative school and university years during which "Watchman" had been composed in order to portray in a romanticized version of himself what by now he had learned about "the high Archangel's call." At school, the sole image in Emerald's window is an angel of sorts: "He is shown the narrow cubicle in which he is to sleep; and there it still is, with nothing else, in the window-pane, as he lies;—'our tower,' the 'Angel Steeple,' noblest of its kind. Here, from morning to night, everything seems challenged to follow the upward lead of its long, bold, 'perpendicular' lines. The very place one is in, its stone-work, its empty spaces, invade you" (*Miscellaneous Studies,* 206–07). This steeple which fills Emerald's window—so called from the angel that originally had surmounted the tower of

Canterbury Cathedral—epitomizes the cultural tradition for
which the King's School stands. Emerald's window-*cum*-
angel is like the "unsuspected window" (*Marius*, 1: 40) of the
visionary scene at the Temple of Aesculapius in *Marius* or the
"windows left ajar unknowingly" (*Miscellaneous Studies*, 181)
in "The Child in the House" (or, in the same portrait, like the
garden gate through which Florian accidentally encounters
the red hawthorn). In a sense Emerald's window also resembles a picture in its frame, like one of Giorgione's "ideal instants . . . which seem to absorb past and future in an intense
consciousness of the present" (*Renaissance*, 150). Emerald's
desire for the atemporality of that visionary moment, which
he pursues through school and army, contrasts with the temporal cycle of his childhood heritage, symbolized by his
buried ancestors who were "sleeping all around under the
windows, deposited there as quietly as fallen trees on their
native soil, and almost unrecorded, as there had been almost
nothing to record" (*Miscellaneous Studies*, 200). Here is a
pagan sensuousness untouched by spiritual aspirations, and
it leaves their consciousness uninscribed: an "almost unrecorded" existence.

This prelinguistic life "under the windows" gives way to
the incessant inscription of the steeple in the window:
Emerald's intellect is the "plain tablet" which lies ready "for
the influences of the place to inscribe" (207); observers find
in his face "the physiognomy of his race; ennobled now, as if
by the writing, the signature, there, of a grave intelligence,
by grave information and a subdued will" (221). Although
"plucked" from the Uthwart world of natural processes,
Emerald nonetheless blossoms anew in this ancient bastion
of learning—a rather more youthful and less decadent Mr.
Rose. In a passage composed at the same time as the portrait
of Emerald, Pater describes all knowledge as a kind of flowering of earlier inscription: "Ancient, half-obliterated in-

scriptions on the mental walls, the mental tablet, seeds of knowledge to come, shed by some flower of it long ago, it was in an earlier period of time they had been laid up in him, to blossom again now, so kindly, so firmly!" (*Plato*, 66). These "ancient, half-obliterated inscriptions" which flowered anew in the mind of the young boy in the *Meno* appear in Emerald's portrait as names inscribed on the tablets of the King's School—in the list of those who for centuries had missed chapel or in Emerald's carved school desk "crowded as an old churchyard with forgotten names" (*Miscellaneous Studies*, 207). The desk as a churchyard of tombstones blends with the image in *Plato* of half-obliterated inscriptions about "to blossom again" to suggest that the intellectual tablet is at one and the same time the gravestone of forgotten selves ("grave intelligence" indeed!) and the seedbed of new life: "the elements of which we are composed . . . are broadcast, driven in many currents; and birth and gesture and death and the springing of violets from the grave are but a few out of ten thousand resultant combinations" (*Renaissance*, 234). So also, in this sense, the stones of Oxford University are "a composite of minute dead bodies" (*Miscellaneous Studies*, 227), and Marius's "city of tombs, layer upon layer of dead things and people," seems almost textually inscribed by "line upon line of successive ages of builders" (*Marius*, 1: 200, 174).

Speaking in "The Child in the House" of the influences which inscribe themselves on consciousness, Pater drew upon widely divergent times and traditions (Locke, Aristotle, Job) to base this image of the mental tablet: "How indelibly, as we afterwards discover, they affect us; with what capricious attractions and associations they figure themselves on the white paper, the smooth wax, of our ingenuous souls, as 'with lead in the rock for ever,' giving form and feature, and as it were assigned house-room in our memory, to early experiences of feeling and thought, which abide with us ever afterwards, thus, and not otherwise" (*Miscellaneous Studies*, 177). For the young lad Florian, "the white paper, the smooth wax" represent consciousness about to become aware of itself through inscription; but because inscription proceeds according to the differential relation of the Dioscuri, it involves a loss of wholeness, a division that creates "a self not himself." The contents of the mind exist as creations of alterity. Describing the basic "difference for the sense, in those whites and reds through the smoke" (175), for the emerging sensibility of the child Florian, Pater hints at a differential relationship which later is made explicit in *Marius*: " 'The red rose came first,' says a quaint German mystic, speaking of 'the mystery of the so-called *white* things,' as being 'ever an afterthought—the doubles, or seconds, of real things, and themselves but half-real, half-material'" (*Marius*, 1: 13). As conjugate variables or creations of alterity, white and red represent the perpetually interchanging states of priority and repetition. The red rose of sensuous experience "came first," inscribing the "white paper" of the child's mind, which then, steeped in the "fire of colour" (*Renaissance*, 221), passes from the white innocence of childhood into the red rose (or "read" text, given the "white paper" with which the process began) of experience, seeking afterward to regain that now decentered wholeness, "half-real, half-material."

That this interplay of Polydeuces and Castor is one of pain is evident in Pater's elaboration of the image of consciousness as "smooth wax." Later in the portrait of Florian, "an older boy taught him to make flowers of sealing-wax, and he had burnt his hand badly at the lighted taper, and been unable to sleep" (*Miscellaneous Studies*, 189). This burning of the hand, which Wright describes as an autobiographical incident, is equivalent to the artist's immersion in the "fire of colour," represented in "The Child in the House" by the flaming red hawthorn. Only the pagan Greeks or Winckelmann and the old Uthwarts remain unsinged:

> Greek sensuousness . . . does not fever the blood; it is shameless and childlike. But Christianity, with its uncompromising idealism, discrediting the slightest touch of sense, has lighted up for the artistic life, with its inevitable sensuousness, a background of flame. "I did but taste a little honey with the end of the rod that was in mine hand, and lo, I must die." It is hard to pursue that life without something of conscious disavowal of a spiritual world; and this imparts to genuine artistic interests a kind of intoxication. From this intoxication Winckelmann is free; he fingers those pagan marbles with unsinged hands, with no sense of shame or loss.[8]

Unlike the "unsinged hands" of the naturally pagan Winckelmann, the badly burned hand of the child Florian testifies to a modern mentality distorted by medieval distrust of the senses. In "Apollo in Picardy," Prior Saint-Jean sees "the white breadth of wall" in his little cell "alight softly; and looking, as he fancied, from the window, saw also a low circlet of soundless flame, waving, licking daintily up the black sky, but harmless, beautiful, closing in upon that round dark space in the midst, which was the earth. He seemed to feel upon his shoulder just then the touch of his friend beside him. 'It is hell-fire!' he said" (146–47).

Like the flame in Prior Saint-Jean's window, beautiful but feared, the angel in Emerald's window proves equally sinister. As fatally as Mr. Archangels, this angel puts a bullet in Emerald's heart; and, at the same time, Emerald's companion James Stokes is slain. Emerald and James are like the brothers Dioscuri, and the distinction between Emerald's fatal bullet

8. Pater, "Winckelmann," *Westminster Review* NS 31 (1867): 104.

and James's is illusory. That common bullet, symbol both of Emerald's guilt (in that he and James were condemned to die by firing squad) and of his heroism (since his old, glorious gunshot wound takes his life), produces the interplay of difference that has replaced childhood wholeness. Within the army, which represents an exaggerated form of school discipline and demands an even greater degree of submission from the naturally submissive Emerald, the spirit can discover no escape from an entrapping environment, no relational interplay between the reds and whites, but encounters only a monotonous white plain of snow. Emerald's and James's one act of self-assertion inscribes that whiteness and enlists against them the full rigor of the law. But that wholeness, now decentered, can yet be regained within the very dialectic which initially had destroyed it. The surgeon who performed the autopsy on Emerald's body remarked in his diary: "I was struck by the great beauty of the organic developments, in the strictly anatomic sense; those of the throat and diaphragm in particular might have been modelled for a teacher of normal physiology, or a professor of design" (245). In the essay on Winckelmann, Pater had noted that the typical ideal of Greek sculpture "unveils man in the repose of his unchanging characteristics. That white light, purged from the angry, bloodlike stains of action and passion, reveals . . . the indifference which lies beyond all that is relative or partial" (*Renaissance*, 213, 218). As he lies there, just before he is enclosed in his coffin, Emerald resembles nothing so much as the ideal of Greek sculpture in its breadth and universality; the stain of blood turned back upon its opposite recaptures that purged whiteness of the lost wholeness.[9]

9. In the multiple reflections and reorderings of meaning that constitute the Paterian use of imagery, the "bloodlike stains" in contrast to the "white light" undoubtedly draws upon the famous fifty-second stanza of Shelley's "Adonais": "The One remains, the many change and pass; / Heaven's light forever shines, Earth's shadows fly; / Life, like a dome of many-coloured

Contemplating, at the opening of the portrait, the epitaph at Siena of a German student, the narrator notes: "Loving parents and elder brother meant to record carefully the very days of the lad's poor life—*annos, menses, dies*; sent the order, doubtless, from the distant old castle in the Fatherland, but not quite explicitly; the spaces for the numbers remain still unfilled; and they never came to see. After two centuries the omission is not to be rectified; and the young man's memorial has perhaps its propriety as it stands, with those unnumbered, or numberless, days" (*Miscellaneous Studies*, 197–98). As the "unnumbered" days become "numberless," so the absence of dates and name on the lid (or tablet) of Emerald's coffin suggests a transcendence of the particularities of time and space. Dying, Emerald has reached the point at which inscription can begin anew, as it had for the "tablet" of Marius's mind, "white and smooth," awaiting "whatsoever divine fingers might choose to write there." Between the opening epitaph with its unfilled spaces and the concluding image of the uninscribed coffin lid, the portrait explores the interplay of difference within sensuous experience. That interplay, perpetually slaying the elder and replacing him with the younger, who then is sacrificed so that once again the elder may be revivified, caused a profound uneasiness in Pater's readers. And society's tendency to deny or fear this entanglement of spirit with matter, of beauty with evil, was met and matched by Pater's corresponding uneasiness as to its personal significance and public repercussions.

Not long after the publication of *The Renaissance*, Pater's

glass, / Stains the white radiance of Eternity, / Until Death tramples it to fragments." Shelley's allusion to stained-glass links Pater's discussion of Winckelmann's imaginative experience both to the countryside of La Beauce as seen from the "incense-laden sanctuary" of Saint Hubert's, "like a many-coloured carpet spread under the great dome, with the white double house-front quivering afar through the heat," and, more generally, to all those dyes and stains of the flux as web or arena.

colleague John Wordsworth had written to him, in what is now a well-known letter, that his dislike of Pater's philosophy of "momentary enjoyment" must "become public and avowed, and it may be my duty to oppose you. . . . Could you indeed have known the dangers into which you were likely to lead minds weaker than your own, you would, I believe, have paused."[10] Continued attacks against him from the pulpit and in print, most notably in Mallock's Peacockian satire, *The New Republic*, led Pater to suppress his Conclusion in the second edition of *The Renaissance* in 1876 because, as he noted, "it might possibly mislead some of those young men into whose hands it might fall" (*Renaissance*, 233). This fear of misleading can be understood most clearly if one considers two other attacks on *The Renaissance* shortly after its publication, both by W. J. Courthope in the *Quarterly Review*: "Modern Culture" (1874) and "Wordsworth and Gray" (1876). In the first essay Pater's description of the Mona Lisa brought down Courthope's wrath for its "epicene" poetic prose, and in the second Pater is seen as the most representative contemporary advocate of an "emasculated" romanticism. Citing passages from the Conclusion, Courthope re-

---

10. *Letters*, ed. Evans, pp. 13–14. Wordsworth closes his letter with a request: "Would you object to give up to myself or to the other tutors (if they will take it) your share in the Divinity Examination in Collections? This . . . would be, I confess, a relief to my mind if you would consent to do so." Wilde's performance at this examination shortly thereafter precisely points up what it was about Pater's philosophy which disturbed Wordsworth: "In his *viva voce* examination for 'Divvers' at Oxford, Oscar Wilde was required to translate from the Greek version of the New Testament, which was one of the set books. The passage chosen was from the story of the Passion. Wilde began to translate, easily and accurately. The examiners were satisfied, and told him that this was enough. Wilde ignored them and continued to translate. After another attempt the examiners at last succeeded in stopping him, and told him that they were satisfied with his translation. 'Oh, do let me go on,' said Wilde, 'I want to see how it ends.' " *The Oxford Book of Literary Anecdotes*, ed. James Sutherland (Oxford: Clarendon, 1975), p. 299.

pudiated (in common "with most Englishmen") "the
effeminate desires which Mr. Pater, the mouthpiece of our
artistic 'culture,' would encourage in society." Given the
climate of undergraduate gossip and public allegations of
sexual deviance, some response beyond the suppression of
the offending Conclusion was necessary; and Pater's initial
reply to Courthope's attack on himself and on "that disease
which we call Romanticism" came as early as his 1876 essay
"Romanticism."[11]

There Pater had replied sharply to those such as Courthope, "critics who would never have discovered for themselves the charm of any work, whether new or old, who value
what is old, in art or literature, for its accessories, and chiefly
for the conventional authority that has gathered about it—
people who would never really have been made glad by any
Venus fresh-risen from the sea, and who praise the Venus of
old Greece and Rome, only because they fancy her grown
now into something staid and tame" (*Appreciations*, 242). Because the romantic spirit is "an ever-present, an enduring
principle, in the artistic temperament" (243), the distinction
is never between a "healthy" reason and an "unhealthy"
passion, old against new, but is between all these qualities in
dynamic interchange over against immobile convention:
"For, in truth, the legitimate contention is, not of one age or
school of literary art against another, but of all successive
schools alike, against the stupidity which is dead to the sub-
stance, and the vulgarity which is dead to form" (261). The

11. Courthope, "Modern Culture," *Quarterly Review* 137 (1874): 411, and
"Wordsworth and Gray," *Quarterly Review* 141 (1876): 132, 136. Courthope's
passion for a "healthy" art and his aversion to an "unhealthy" aestheticism
found support in other periodical broadsides, notably Leslie Stephen, "Art
and Morality," *Cornhill Magazine* 32 (1875): 91–101. An interesting
defense of Pater is to be found in "Essays and Notices," *Contemporary Review* 30 (1877): 1099, in which he is seen as the "scapegoat" of those who
dislike aestheticism.

"stupidity" and "vulgarity" of Courthope's dogmatic opinions are as dead as the epitaphs, hieroglyphics, and reliquaries in which absolutists of every age try to fix the truth. Afterward, in both *Marius* and *Gaston*, Pater alluded to Courthope's false opposition between classic and romantic (Pater probably did not know the identity of his anonymous adversary in the *Quarterly* who, a few years younger than Pater himself, certainly was "elderly" only in his state of mind): "Elderly people, Virgil in hand, might assert professionally that the contemporary age, an age, of course, of little people and things, deteriorate since the days of their own youth, must necessarily be unfit for poetic uses" (*Gaston*, 52–53); and, "Certain elderly counsellors, filling what may be thought a constant part in the little tragi-comedy which literature and its votaries are playing in all ages, would ask, suspecting some affectation or unreality in that minute culture of *form*:—Cannot those who have a thing to say, say it directly? Why not be simple and broad, like the old writers of Greece?" (*Marius*, 1: 99).

Significantly, when in 1889 Pater republished "Romanticism" as the Postscript to *Appreciations*, he presumably feared Baudelaire's reputation as "unhealthy" and suppressed all mention of his name in that essay, substituting Hugo's in its place. Whereas in 1876 he had dared to defend and praise Baudelaire as the embodiment of romanticism, by 1889 it had become obvious that Baudelaire's flowers of evil were regarded with continuing, even growing, hostility by "most Englishmen" and that no defense could absolve him or Pater of decadence. Emerald and, after him, Prior Saint-Jean offer poignant testimony to Pater's increasingly despairing realization that for him also animosity and misinterpretation would never pass into forgiveness and approval except across the untranslatable gap of death.

Less than a year before his death, Pater published "Apollo in Picardy," a culminating statement by him on his own art. A fictional portrait about the rediscovery in France of the "Gothic" or romantic spirit, its hero, Prior Saint-Jean, is a monk who is revitalized by a medieval Apollo-in-exile. Here for the final and climactic time in Pater's writings the ambiguous angel appears; for Apollo is called by the name of "a malignant one in Scripture, Apollyon" (*Miscellaneous Studies*, 152), described in Revelation 9:11 as the angel of the bottomless pit. Staying for his health with his young companion, Hyacinth, at a monastic grange, the prior under Apollyon's tuition transforms the twelfth and final volume of his great treatise on mathematics into an exotic celebration of sensuous beauty: images of lights, stars, and colors. In "Prior Saint-Jean's folly," as it is called, there may even be a hint of Pater's Conclusion, for both the prior's and Pater's concluding statements destroyed the chances of promotion for their authors. After accidentally killing Hyacinth with a discus, Apollyon vanishes and leaves the prior wrongly accused of the boy's death. The grieving prior spends his last days confined to a room from which he can glimpse (almost like Saint John after whom he is named) the new heaven and new earth of the senses to which he desires to return. Though the prior in a number of essentials is certainly different from Pater, the plight of a writer unable to finish his great life's work must have been inescapable to Pater who at this time was surely himself discovering that his projected trilogy would never be completed.

Apollyon's world of the senses, of flux, of the earth and its generation and decay, which the prior and his brethren initially found so threatening, had for Pater a very personal relevance. In the prior, conservative, provincial, moralistic, pure, idealistic, and in Apollyon, naturalistic, sensuous, pagan, Pater sketched a paradigm of the young Oxford scholar's ruinous encounter with Baudelaire's flowers of evil—or at least with nineteenth-century French romanticism. Initially, the prior shudders at the world of nature and its "flowers" (145), and he keeps his distance from "the whole crew of miscreant poets" (146); the beautiful Apollyon must, the prior feels, be "spotted with unseen evil" (149) and the unspoiled paradise of the monks' valley haunted by a "'secret evil'" (150). But at the end of the portrait, it is the color of the hyacinths—and the dead lad who has become the blue flowers—which the prior, by now regarded by others as mad, has learned to love and toward which he is irresistibly drawn. In this, the prior's collapse parallels Pater's own failure to surmount his private sense of loss at having slain "the old, immemorial, well-recognised types in art and literature" by "an original, untried *matter*, still in fusion" (*Appreciations*, 257–58) and also his failure to justify himself publicly, to explain those *fleurs* of romanticism to society.

As with so many of Pater's short portraits which begin with an imaginary discovery or unveiling of some text, "Apollo" postulates the recovery of the prior's manuscript "from an old monastic library in France at the Revolution" (*Miscellaneous Studies*, 143). That it should turn up at the French Revolution is significant, for this was a period of change, a time of radical social transformation in which the new replaced the old. In "A Prince of Court Painters" and "Romanticism" Pater had characterized this overthrow of the ancien régime as a storm—the sort of storm which in "Sebastian" altered the landscape and which in "Apollo" at the conclusion blew up at the death of Hyacinth. This rejuvenating, romantic tempest is summoned by Apollyon who symbolizes the Dioscuri-like unity of the prior and his filial half, Hyacinth. At Apollyon's withdrawal (like the flight of Cupid or the absent Zeus) the ideal unity is split, and the

prior's text, which had been transformed by the presence of
Apollyon (much as Denys had inspired the illustration of the
Ovid at the monastery at Auxerre), is now abandoned.
Clearly, the prior's sort of work, "a dry enough treatise" (143)
not unlike Aurelius's dryly systematic exposition, needed
some renewal; and the influence of Apollyon upon the study
should not be seen as negative.

Earlier, in such rigid "classical" efforts as Sebastian's
journal, Pater had coupled the tendency to seek absolute
Truth with the characteristically inflexible form of the
treatise. In *Plato* he had declared:

> The treatise, as the instrument of a dogmatic philoso-
> phy *begins* with an axiom or definition: the essay or
> dialogue, on the other hand, as the instrument of
> dialectic, does not necessarily so much as conclude in
> one; like that long dialogue with oneself, that dialectic
> process, which may be co-extensive with life. It does
> in truth little more than clear the ground, as we say, or
> the atmosphere, or the mental tablet, that one may
> have a fair chance of knowing, or seeing, perhaps: it
> does but put one into a duly receptive attitude to-
> wards such possible truth, discovery, or revelation, as
> may one day occupy the ground, the tablet,—shed it-
> self on the purified air; it does not provide a proposi-
> tion, nor a system of propositions, but forms a temper.
> [*Plato*, 188]

The idea of the essay and its dialectic that clears the "mental
tablet" harks back to Marius's "tablet of the mind white and
smooth" and to the nameless and dateless coffin lid of
Emerald. Within this dialectic there is no final "proposition," only the perpetual turning back of one pole upon the
other, establishing sufficient continuity and duration within
the flux to enable consciousness to move from one moment to

the next. The prior's effort to "arrest" "on the written or printed page" the "beam of insight" (*Miscellaneous Studies,* 164) is akin to Marius's desire to "arrest" "certain clauses of experience" and to live "in a fragment of perfect expression" (*Marius,* 2: 155). But the prior's vision is incommensurate with any textual form known to him, "dividing hopelessly against itself the well-ordered kingdom of his thought" (*Miscellaneous Studies,* 143). Failing to resolve the antagonistic doppelgänger by means of a reflexive structure, the prior's vision overflows the walls of his brain, his room, his garden even: "If he set hand to the page, the firm halo, here a moment since, was gone, had flitted capriciously to the wall; passed next through the window, to the wall of the garden; was dancing back in another moment upon the innermost walls of one's own miserable brain, to swell there—that astounding white light!—rising steadily in the cup, the mental receptacle, till it overflowed, and he lay faint and drowning in it" (164). The treatise abruptly breaks off with an unfinished word as the prior's "hand collapses" and he becomes "his old unimpassioned monastic self once more" (165). Like Botticelli's Madonna whose hand lacked the passion to inscribe her words in the book, the prior also stands in need of that dialectical interplay of his existence with the next frame out—the authorial level of inscription. Significantly, his treatise "could never be bound" (144); for, apart from its physical form, its perceptions remain hopelessly divided, unharmonized, unstructured.

In the collapse of the prior, a reflection may be perceived of the creative crisis Pater seems to have faced about 1887–88, which had the abandonment of *Gaston de Latour* as its main consequence. After the surge of activity in which *Marius, Imaginary Portraits,* and several of the essays for *Appreciations* had been composed and in which *Gaston* had been begun, Pater's lifelong debility of will, that "weariness of the way"

(181) which beset Florian, seems suddenly to have overwhelmed him. This may be glimpsed even in a detail such as
Pater's handwriting which, the editor of his letters observes,
"changes appreciably over the course of his adult life. . . .
From the stiff verticality of the 1860s . . . evolves a graceful
script that does not alter appreciably from about 1870 to
about 1887. . . . In the later eighties, however, the handwriting begins to grow irregular and slovenly, at first during
intervals when Pater was evidently plagued by attacks of
gout, and eventually as a matter of course."[12] Pater himself
regarded the handwriting in letters as something of a key to
personality. William Sharp reports that he once remarked to
him: " 'Imagine the pleasure of reading the intimate letters
of Michael Angelo, of Giorgione, of Lionardo, of Dante, of
Spenser, of Shakespeare, of Goethe, in the originals! It would
be like looking on a landscape in clear sunlight or moonlight,
after having viewed it only through mist or haze.' "[13] The
deterioration of Pater's script may not be owing simply to
gout or to a latent, ultimately fatal, rheumatic fever; rather,
the collapsing hand may reflect the paralyzing blow of his
brother William's death.

In 1887, between the first serial publications of "Denys
l'Auxerrois" and "Duke Carl of Rosenmold," Pater's brother
died at the end of a "long and trying illness."[14] The appearance of *Imaginary Portraits* on 24 May, only one month after
his decease, came too hard upon the event for Pater to dedi-
cate the volume to William's memory. The following year,
publication of *Gaston* began and ignominiously ended. But a
year after abandoning *Gaston*, Pater's 1889 *Appreciations*—
which included the retitled "Romanticism" as its Postscript—bore a tribute: "To the memory of my brother /

12. *Letters,* ed. Evans, pp. xliii–iv.
13. Sharp, "Personal Reminiscences," p. 805.
14. *Letters,* ed. Evans, p. 72.

William Thompson Pater / Who quitted a useful and happy
life / Sunday April 24 1887 / Requiem eternam dona ei
Domine / Et lux perpetua luceat ei." Wright's comment
that to Pater the blow of William's death "had been a crushing one, for . . . like the brothers in *Gaston de Latour*, written the following year, they had been 'perfect friends,' "
unwittingly may have supplied the key to Pater's failure, despite repeated efforts, to finish his autobiographical trilogy.[15] Like the dying elder brother who also functioned as a
surrogate father for the poet-to-be in "Joachim du Bellay" (an
earlier study set in the same era as *Gaston*), the death of Pater's handsome and envied older brother undoubtedly lead
Pater in *Gaston* and afterward in "Emerald" and "Apollo" to
a textual interpretation of the myth of Polydeuces and Castor.
If Pater's superego could not condone the ambivalent or hostile feelings toward William which originated in competition
for the mother's affection, his private guilt might be exor-
cised in the public arena of literary creation. There the elder
brother-father, in the form of a rigid classicism (text or critic),
is slain so that the younger, as autobiographical author of his
life, might himself possess that paternity for which he insatiably yearned.

However, by the later eighties the public drama could *not*
exorcise the private guilt but could only compound it. With
his decadent disciples on the one hand and the hostile critics
on the other, there could be no Dioscuri-like dialectic to
bring forth a filial critic capable of understanding Pater. The
figure of Apollyon on the gable of the grange, "with an ugly
gap between the shoulder and the fingers on the harp, as if,
literally, he had cut off his right hand and put it from him"
(154), epitomizes Pater's plight. The gospel text here describes the temptation to sin as the reason for cutting off the
hand. Although "the sword in the world, the right eye

15. Wright, *Pater*, 2: 99.

plucked out, the right hand cut off, the spirit of reproach which those images express, and of which monasticism is the fulfilment, reflect one side only of the nature of the divine missionary of the New Testament" (*Marius*, 2: 114), Apollyon's missing arm signifies an unusually strong determination by the prior's monastic colleagues to repress natural impulse. Unable to play his harp, Apollyon denotes not only the prior's inability to finish the treatise but also Pater's failure to complete his trilogy. That Apollo's silver harp (not golden because a hyperborean moonlight has replaced the sunlight of ancient Greece) is actually the author's text would be evident apart from his function as the patron of the muses, but it becomes especially manifest when it is found unstrung at the bottom of the pigeon house "on the sanded floor, soaking in the pale milky blood and torn plumage" (*Miscellaneous Studies*, 160) of the slaughtered birds. This imagery turns back to the red patches on the sand of the arena and the reconstitution of the self in textual terms. In the light of *Marius*, the broken strings of Apollyon's harp should be read as the deconstructed text—even, perhaps, as the lines of type across the page disarranged. In this there is a similarity with Duke Carl and his plan to actualize the theme of Conrad Celtes's Ode by bringing Apollo with his lyre to Germany—an effort to invigorate, with the help of his son Goethe, a sterile classicism. The portrait of Carl had opened with an image of his bones and those of his bride found "much distorted, and lying . . . in great confusion" (*Imaginary Portraits*, 119). Distorted bones within the soil or broken strings upon the sanded floor—each is a prelude to an Apollonian ideal of beauty created, lost, and re-created generation after generation by the ambiguous angel of art.

But owing to an imputation of guilt, Courthope and his ilk have figuratively broken off the writer's arm, making it impossible for Pater to continue his work. In terms of the

textual significance of the Dioscuri, this absence of Apollo's
inspiration is the condition of the mortal Castor "breathing
his last," the condition of a hidebound intellectual classicism
in which the prior and Pater are checked by society's disap-
proval of the romantic flowers of art. The secret of the recovery of the absent creative energy is the perpetual sacrifice
of Hyacinth for the prior and of the prior for Hyacinth. The
grave, prepared for "the body of an ancient villager" (*Miscellaneous Studies*, 166), becomes instead the one in which the
youth Hyacinth will be laid. As in the portrait of Denys an
emerald green flask heralding the coming of a golden age was
found within the grave, so in "Apollo" the discovery in the
graveyard of a pagan discus (symbol of the seasonal cycle, of
transformation) heralds a renewal through death, for the instrument which kills Hyacinth also embodies by its "perpetual motion" (167) a redemption from death by change.
Like the beautiful girl found preserved "from corruption and
the injury of time" in a Roman sarcophagus[16] or like Pico
who remains "as one alive in the grave" (*Renaissance,* 49) or
like the youth of humanity itself "still red with life in the
grave" (209), Hyacinth descends into the grave-as-womb to
be reborn, not only as the blue flowers but as the blue "of
Holy Mary's gown on the illuminated page, the colour of
hope, of merciful omnipresent deity" (*Miscellaneous Studies,*
170–71). As in *Marius,* so here the Hyacinthus myth signifies
a passage through blood to become the words or pictures on
the page, the page itself coalescing with the angel-figure,
"Holy Mary."

In "Diaphanéité," Pater had remarked of his crystal hero
that "Poetry and poetical history have dreamed of a crisis,
where it must needs be that some human victim be sent down
into the grave. These are they whom in its profound emotion
humanity might choose to send" (253). Through the mutual

16. Pater, "Symonds's 'Renaissance in Italy,' " *Uncollected Essays* (Port-
land, Maine: T. B. Mosher, 1903), p. 8.

annihilation of Hyacinth in the prior, of subject in object, of romantic in classic, of matter in form, such sacrifice closes the "ugly gap" between "untranslatable" "ultimate differences" and constitutes the restoration of godlike wholeness. As each dies for the sake of the other—as the origin and its repetition are perpetually turned back upon each other—Polydeuces' prayer to lie in the grave in his brother's stead is answered. In this the prior and Hyacinth, as creations of alterity, are each in turn the father and the son; for, as fixed origins dissolve in dialectical repetitions, "all things are at once old and new"; thus, for example, "in the products of Greek civilisation, the actual elements are traceable elsewhere, . . . yet all is also emphatically *autochthonous,* as the Greeks said, new-born at home" (*Greek Studies,* 215–16). So, too, in the ceaselessly alternating antinomies of creator and created a dialectic is revealed between the classical text fostering a maturing talent and a reciprocal romantic re-creation of that text through a surrender or relinquishing of the self to literature. The prior, whose title as an adjective betokens his status as the "former" or "earlier in time," aspires to the final rank of abbot (or "father," which also is the meaning of Pater's name); but instead of becoming the originating father he becomes "simple Brother, Saint-Jean" (*Miscellaneous Studies,* 170)—his priority and paternity yielding to the repetition of the Dioscuri by which Hyacinth, his son, becomes the father. The permission for the prior to return to the valley of the monks comes only at his death, a prelude to Hyacinth's return in the next frame out as the father (that is, as Pater the author).

In the final analysis, the ugly gap of Apollyon's missing hand signifies not merely society's repression of the author but the writer's own covert complicity in his persecution as atonement for his primitive parricidal aggression. It is certainly significant that in his earliest published essay, "Coleridge's Writings," Pater should invoke the image of

Stephen, the first Christian martyr: "Stephen's face, 'like the face of an angel,' has a worth of its own, even if the opened heaven is but a dream."[17] Stoned to death, Stephen "kneeled down, and cried with a loud voice, Lord, lay not this sin to their charge" (Acts 7: 60). Echoing, as it does, the vicious "stomping" Pater received midway through his school years at Canterbury and his sickbed plea that the offender not be expelled, which the headmaster took to be a magnanimous act of Christian forbearance, this suggests that the stones that kill Stephen, like the flying discus that destroys Hyacinth, are for the author the necessary price of pardon. This paradoxically redemptive yet mutilating aspect of inscription is clearly present also at the structural and thematic center of *Marius* in the image of the burned hand, an analogue to Apollyon's broken, missing arm: "Scaevola might watch his own hand, consuming, crackling, in the fire, in the person of a culprit, willing to redeem his life by an act so delightful to the eyes, the very ears, of a curious public" (*Marius*, 1: 239). The condemned criminal—and "we are all *condamnés*" (*Renaissance*, 238), says Pater—becomes the legendary hero (Scaevola) by repeating the hand-destroying act that saved the Romans. Because the act of inscription decenters every "opened heaven" or ground of origin, the son simultaneously deconstructs the angelic-paternal hand as he reaches out to usurp it, causing a future son to disarm him even as he displaces—*vide* the Christ child guiding the hand of the Madonna or Marius taking dictation from Flavian—the hand of his predecessor. Heroically reconstituted as the textual angel, the author has already yielded his priority, with guilt-atoning forgiveness, to the son in the next frame out who stands on the sidelines like Saul, not yet Paul, keeping the garments of those who hurl the stones.

17. Pater, "Coleridge's Writings," p. 126. Pater's quotation is from Acts 6: 15.

Pater, by surrendering his life to words, renews Hyacinth as a father but does so in the hope that this future life turned into words will purge his own guilt. Yet just as death comes to the prior awaiting the forgiving word which would ensure his return to the valley—like Marius awaiting inscription by the "divine fingers"—so Pater has begun to surmise the bitter truth that the reader-critic of his texts will appear only following his death. Indeed, Pater's efforts to guarantee favorable reviews of his work and his gratitude toward those who commented upon it sympathetically may have little to do with the promotion of his popular reputation but much to do with avoiding misinterpretations that foster lasting confusion as to which Paterides are bastard, which legitimate. Plagued by false sons—the tribe of decadents— Pater longs for a privileged relationship which will reweave and complete his unfinished autobiographical trilogy as in his imaginary portrait he had rewoven and so completed the prior's unfinished, unbound manuscript. Yet just as the prior's expository treatise is reset in a fictional form by Pater, so Pater's fictionalized autobiography can be finished only in some other form—by, one may say merely in way of illustration, a critical discussion of its themes such as may be found in the preceding pages of this study. But in the 1890s, after the bittersweet *fleurs* of those aesthetes who carried the banner of art for art's sake and celebrated Pater's writings as the ultimate expression of that slogan, the father acquiesced in the emasculation implicit in the broken arm. To escape his perilous paternity, Pater undertook a more impersonal work (his *most* impersonal work) that competed with *Gaston* for his attention: the series of lectures in 1891–92 which he published in 1893 as *Plato and Platonism*. There he stressed an increasingly constrained morality, clearly distancing himself from hedonistic excess. *Plato* could be finished as could such shorter portraits as "Emerald" and "Apollo" which, although

drawing on personal experience, were not precisely what
Pater in "The Child in the House" had called "the story of his
spirit" (*Miscellaneous Studies*, 173). And so *Gaston* stands, fragments shored against the ruins of a never-realized autobiographical fantasy, testimony to a guilt its author could not
appease.

# Index